Christian Countermoves In A Decadent Culture

Christian Countermoves In A Decadent Culture

CARL F. H. HENRY

MULTNOMAH · PRESS
Portland, Oregon 97266

Edited by Steve Halliday and Rodney L. Morris
Cover design and illustration by Britt Taylor Collins

CHRISTIAN COUNTERMOVES IN A DECADENT CULTURE
© 1986 by Multnomah Press
Portland, Oregon 97266

Printed in the United States of America

Library of Congress Cataloging-in-Publication Data

Henry, Carl Frederick Howard, 1913-
   Christian countermoves in a decadent culture.
   1. Theology. 2. Sermons, American. I. Title.
BR85.H549   1986   230'.044   86-5286
ISBN 0-88070-151-X

86 87 88 89 90 91 92 93 94 – 10 9 8 7 6 5 4 3 2 1

Contents

PART 1

THE PROBLEM

The God of the Bible and Moral Foundations

*I*t is impossible to contemplate traditional Western values without reference to the God of the Bible. The ideals that lifted the West above ancient paganism had their deepest source and support in the self-revealed God who was and is for Christians the *summum bonum* or supreme good.

Nowhere is the singular uniqueness of the God of the Bible more evident than in the Christian vision of the good and the right that Scripture commends and nurtures. One need only recall the biblical basis of many long-accepted beliefs about the moral order. Among these are the convictions that God is intrinsically moral and the sovereign source of all ethical distinctions; that a comprehensive moral purpose pervades all human history; that the articulately-revealed will of the Creator embraces all matters private and public (including human relationships to fellow humans, to the state, and to the cosmos); that agape is both the nature of God and the prime human virtue; that life even in the womb is God's gift, and that human existence gains its fixed worth from creation in the *imago Dei*; that Jesus of

A paper presented at the opening session of the Christian Studies Convocation, 7 October 1984, sponsored by the Hillsdale College Center for Constructive Alternatives.

Nazareth incarnates the very life, truth, and holy love of God; that the kingdom of God and its blessings are mercifully accessible to sinful humanity through the crucified and risen Jesus who controls the sluice gates of eternity; and that through its unyielding call to the justice and justification of God, the regenerate church as the New Society is to reflect worldwide the joys and privileges of the kingdom of God through its witness to redemptive good news and new life.

The God of the Bible is the self-revealing infinite Spirit. He is the sovereign source of all other being. He is the authoritative and purposive ruler of nature and history, the specifier of a worthy way of life, and ordainer of the community of faith. He stands at the commencement of a flawlessly created cosmos, one which at every stage of its origination he as its Maker declares to be good. When a subsequently rebellious race seeks in Adam autonomously to redefine truth and the good, he mercifully offers salvation; in the incarnate Logos or Second Adam he provides redemption for the penitent. He is the God of holy love. At the end of world history he will stand victorious amid the Omega-fortunes of the nations and of mankind, and in final judgment he will decisively doom evil and eternally vindicate righteousness.

Now and again in the long history of speculative thought, philosophers have vigorously disputed one or another perfection that the Bible predicates of the living God. During the last century, for example, novel metaphysical theories called into question virtually every facet of the Christian definition of God. Philosophers debated whether God is personal, whether he is infinite, whether he is distinct from the cosmos, whether he is unchanging, whether he is all-powerful and all-knowing and all-wise, whether he transcends time, whether he is loving, and even in what sense he may be regarded as the God of truth.

But in the recent past, humanists (as many naturalists now prefer to call themselves) have boldly repudiated God's very existence as a transcendent, personal Being. When John Dewey deplored supernaturalism a generation ago as a noxious faith and proposed replacing Judeo-Christian religion by naturalistic humanism,[1] he nonetheless confusingly retained the term *God* for the interaction between the ideal and actual. The more recent contemporary humanist Paul Kurtz, however, urges us to "weed out permanently the idea of God."[2]

Naturalism reduces all reality to impersonal processes and events. It assails not simply this or that particular article of Christian belief, but rejects the very possibility of a credible theistic faith. Naturalism mythologizes the basic theses of biblical theism, namely, God, creation, revelation, redemption, and judgment.

Because nontheistic world views have now pervasively penetrated contemporary culture—most notably public education, the mass media, and political decision—belief in the God of the Bible no longer governs the Western intellectual's conceptions of truth and goodness, nor does it shape contemporary society's view of liberty and love, or of responsibility and right. Although contemporary humanists champion an agenda of social ethics, their proposals involve little more than a pirating of selected aspects of biblical morality totally unrelated to a naturalistic theory of the universe.

Earlier in this century the historian F. A. Foakes-Jackson remarked that all the West's distinctive virtues stem from the evangelical theology of the Cross. The current revolt against a supernaturally-grounded morality therefore poses something of an enigma for contemporary ethical theory. Philosophical skepticism and moral relativism have engulfed ever wider reaches of modern life until a sweeping civilizational crisis now overshadows the West. Not only do theorists, who try to sustain moral imperatives independently of God, disagree over the ultimate sanction of morals, but they also fail to provide any truly objective basis for their conclusions about the good and the right. Naturalism's inability to sustain fixed ethical principles is nowhere more apparent than in its many contradictory attempts since the Renaissance to fashion a humanistic ethics and in its increasing tendency to justify and even to praise immorality.

In the biblical outlook, God as the Creator of all existence and Lord of life gives a unifying focus to human thought and action. Only in the context of the living God and of his moral purpose in the universe do we find the reason for man's being. "If God, the creator, is," Emil Brunner remarks, "then the gloomy idea of fate and fatality which lies like a spell over the ancient as well as the modern world, loses its basis. It is not a fate, an impersonal abstract determining power . . . which is above everything that is and happens, but He, the creator spirit, the creator person."[3] In consequence, as Arthur F. Holmes observes, biblical monotheism "involves a theology and an ethic that affected every kind of human activity."[4]

To be sure, even the polytheistic gods were viewed by the ancients as trafficking in ethical concerns. But, as Nahum Sarna observes, these gods were "innately capricious": "their ethical quality was but one of many diverse and contradictory attributes and was neither inherent in the idea of the godhead nor absolute." By contrast, says Sarna, morality and ethics "constitute the very essence" of the God of the Bible; his transcendent "thou shalt not" permeates all human history brought into being by the Creator's sovereign will.[5]

In the Bible, God is himself the Good and he declares his original creation to be essentially good. God's commandments articulate and summarize his will for his creatures, and by this righteous standard he judges all people and nations. He predicates our destiny in eternity on our response to his law and to Jesus Christ "the just and holy one."

For Plato, the good was independent of God and was normative for the Demiurge who (according to Plato) gave form to the universe.[6] But for the Bible nothing is absolutely independent of God; everything is dependent on him. Augustine, Duns Scotus, and the Protestant Reformers insisted that God himself decrees the good. Luther affirmed that what God wills "is not right because He ought or was bound, so to will; on the contrary, what takes place must be right because He so wills it."[7] Some of the early modern philosophers—notably Descartes, Locke, and Berkeley—also affirmed divine command morality. As for the neo- orthodox theologians Karl Barth and Emil Brunner, they, too, formally retained a divine command ethics but muted its propositional content by correlating the divine confrontational demand with private faith and decision.

Modern philosophy, for which the nature and then the very existence of God became problematical, increasingly disavowed divine command ethics. John Stuart Mill and J.M.E. McTaggart rejected biblical theism in part because it affirms that the good is what God wills. Today even many professing theists no longer consider the statement that "God wills" something, to be an ethical pronouncement. Divine command morality is even identified with a "might is right" mentality. The current view— shared by many mediating theologians—is, as Jeffrey Stout observes, that morality is autonomous; it is "logically independent from both theoretical reason and theology."[8]

This revolt against the Christian heritage has meant the loss both of an ethically-significant view of God and of a stable morality. Recent modern attempts to ground ethics in intuition or in utility or some other sociological factor merely collapse morality into psychology. If applied consistently to ethics, naturalism erodes any external foundation of morality and reduces values to subjectivity. Ethical claims become merely culture-relative, for an evolving humanity decides what truth and morality signify at any moment.

So confused is the contemporary pursuit of moral imperatives that academics are probing and discussing divine command morality anew for light on the loss of an objective ethic. G.E.M. Anscombe, for example, declares that morality is indispensably rooted in the presuppositions of biblical theism; indeed, she insists, obligation statements make sense only in a divine law conception of ethics.[9] Janinè Marie Idziak has recently gathered essays, some previously untranslated, that promote and defend the traditional view.[10] Erstwhile champions of natural law theory are being confronted by their contemporaries with the biblical emphasis that the law of God is an articulate revelatory provision.

What distinguished ancient Israel from her pagan neighbor nations in the Near East was her knowledge of the revealed will of Yahweh and her commitment to live responsibly in view of his divine commandments. In contrast with Hittite, Egyptian, Babylonian, Canaanite, and Philistine cultures, there arose in consequence, as Eric Voegelin remarks, "a new society, set off from the civilizations of the age" and "living toward a goal beyond history. . . . Here was a people that began its existence in history with a radical leap in being," one that reverses the postulations of social evolution, according to which "a society is supposed to start from primitive myths and advance gradually," whereas Israel began "where a respectable society has difficulties even ending."[11] The supposedly superior modern view that God is answerable to moral norms approved by an evolved and enlightened humanity, has led by contrast to the ethical collapse of contemporary civilization and to moral futility.

Among the great world religions, only Judaism, Christianity, and Islam depict the deity as the sovereign God who speaks intelligibly, a doctrine that Islam, moreover, clearly inherited from the Judeo-Christian Scriptures. Secular philosophy, even where it champions speculative theism, is hostile to this emphasis on transcendent, rational revelation in order to advance philosophical reasoning as an alternative way of knowing metaphysical and moral reality. But speculative philosophy has bred logically contradictory views, and now even obscures the very meaning of meaning. The recent past has spawned irrational philosophies and religions, most notably existentialism and mysticism. It tells much about such modern alternatives that their most vigorous complaint against the biblical heritage is that orthodox theism appeals for cognitive consent and logical consistency.

The God of the Bible communicates his thought and word intelligibly. He addresses the human mind and conscience through external nature and history, universally confronting humanity's sullied but still surviving *imago Dei* with the knowledge of his transcendent divinity (Romans 1:18ff.), and reminding sinful mankind that the human revolt against light invites inescapable judgment (Romans 1:32). God makes known his character and will not only in general or universal revelation, but specifically in his salvific disclosure to his covenant people; this he does, moreover, both in redemptive historical acts and in the inspired and inscripturated prophetic-apostolic interpretation of those acts, and supremely so in the divine incarnation in Jesus Christ.

This fact, of God's articulate disclosure of his moral will—published both in the Decalogue and in other ethical imperatives in Scripture as well as that published in the life and ministry of Jesus Christ—has far-reaching consequences. It disputes mystics who would deny intelligibility to divine revelation because of its supernatural character. And it disputes modern rationalists as well, who in the name of evolutionary intelligence consider final, divine revelation offensive to the modern mind. No one should be surprised that such commentators, shrouding God as they do in metaphysical obscurity, often propound mythopoetical views of revelation. Nor should we find it incredible that this defamation of divine disclosure involves, in turn, a loss of the ontological foundations of Christian faith.

The Bible teaches that the one living and self-disclosed God is all-wise and self-consistent. This doctrine of the unity, wisdom, and self-consistency of God "was impressed upon Western civilization," says John Jefferson Davis, "only after a long and arduous struggle with Greek, Roman, and barbarian polytheism."[12] In our own time, novel theories of divinity are once again disputing divine wisdom and self-consistency, tenets of great importance to basic aspects of Judeo-Christian doctrine such as revelation, creation, providence, redemption, and eschatology. Process theology views God as a divinity growing in knowledge. Its insistence that God is an aspect of all reality leads, moreover, to the notion that divinity striates even the realm of evil. Dialectical theology views God as a deity who eludes rational synthesis; emphasizing an inner divine command, it deprives the biblical commandments of their proper status as rational, propositional revelation. It is impossible, from such views, to derive a comprehensive, intelligibly-consistent outlook either on God's essential moral nature or on the ideal content of the moral life.

The biblical view insistently declares God to be the sole sovereign of the universe: creator, preserver, governor, and judge. The Decalogue (Exodus 20) relates all the ethical demands impinging upon man and society to the will and purpose of the one living God. The implications of God's universal sovereignty extend to every sphere of life and thought.

The dominion over nature that God has assigned to man (Genesis 1:26; Psalm 8:6) entails human sensitivity to the Creator's moral and spiritual purposes for our planet. It is this biblical emphasis on human dominion that secular theories at times have unjustifiably blamed for the plunder and exploitation of natural resources. Christians may not always have fully implemented ecological responsibilities, but they have at least identified the moral framework that objectively motivates conscience and action. Naturalistic morality, on the other hand, can neither summon nor vindicate fixed ethical principles of any kind. If *homo sapiens* is essentially but an animal, he can hardly be expected to subordinate self-interest to the good of the community. For that reason, even as Christians have brought to the ad hoc concern of secular nature-lovers a depth and permanence of protest against cosmic pollution that mere humanism cannot sustain, so now they must also speak up against the littering of outer space by satellite and missile debris.

The implications of divine sovereignty, we said, are far-reaching. Take, for example, the political realm. Aristotle held that human beings—at least in the sphere of politics—belong to the state, a misunderstanding that no scripturally-grounded Jew or Christian would hesitate to challenge. According to the Bible, the state exists within God's providential will and has limited authority. When totalitarian states presume to define human rights and duties at will, they illicitly claim divine prerogatives. The state's biblically stated role is to maintain God-ordained justice, not to devise or manipulate it; as the American charter political documents declare, human beings are endowed by their Creator with certain inalienable rights. Sad to say, the United Nations Declaration of Human Rights obscures this emphasis on the transcendent supernatural foundation and stipulation of human rights; it does so, moreover, precisely at a time in history when monstrous totalitarian claims are being made by predatory powers.

Religious freedom—that is, one's right to worship and to obey God in good conscience—shelters and nurtures all other human rights, and in this sense undergirds them. Only if human beings have political and civil liberty to worship according to conscience can they worship and serve the living God meaningfully and resist the efforts of arbitrary powers who require subjects to do what God prohibits or to abstain from what God requires. In the absence of individual liberty to worship conscientiously, citizens fall prey to pretentious powers that arrogate to themselves the absolute authority and unqualified honor reserved only to God. The example of the Christian apostles, who when thwarted by civil authorities in fulfilling the Great Commission preferred physical imprisonment to spiritual disobedience ("We must obey God rather than men!" Acts 5:29), remains normative for Christians even today.

Humanists hostile to revealed religion frequently cite instances of gross intolerance and persecution within the course of religious history such as the ancient Hebrew extinction of pagan neighbors in the name of Yahweh, the medieval Crusades, the Inquisition, and even the religious wars of recent modern times, including Islam's reliance on the sword to extend Muhammadan influence. This lamentable record is not offset simply by noting that the Bible nowhere exonerates persecutors that darken the annals of Christendom, be they nonbelievers or believers.

We should remind humanist critics, however, that world history records no persecution and inhumanity more debased and cruel than that waged against theists and dissenters under the banner of atheistic philosophies and rulers. Examples include the Hitler regime's murder of six million Jews and vast numbers of Gentiles, Stalin's destruction of some fifteen million Russians, and Mao's approved murder of some twenty-five million Chinese. Nothing in the entire history of mankind can match this twentieth-century brutality, in a time frame that scientific naturalism extols for its technocratic genius and as the pinnacle of human progress.

Religious freedom is in fact and in essence a Christian priority. It should say something to all world religions that in the United States, which has no state religion, voluntary religion has nurtured a predominantly theistic citizenry whose vigorous evangelistic and humanitarian outreach to the world is unrivaled among the nations.

God's love in the biblical model has nurtured and unleashed a veritable floodtide of compassion in human history. In Judeo-Christian Scripture, divine love is not *eros* or interest in an object for self-serving ends, but rather *agape,* an outgoing affection that confers upon the needy an unmerited benefit. The supreme example of agape is the Father's salvific gift of the divine Son and Redeemer: "For God so loved the world that he gave his one and only Son, that whoever believes in him shall not perish but have eternal life" (John 3:16). Every one of the extended references to divine agape in the New Testament epistles focuses on the Cross, that is, on the Savior's substitutionary atonement for sinners.

The agape of God, as Anders Nygren remarks, "reverses natural human valuation."[13] That Christ died for us while we were yet sinners and in fact enemies of God has injected into human relationships a motivation that neither speculative philosophy nor empirical science nor humanistic education has managed to engender or maintain. Biblical theism has stimulated an unprecedented manifestation of compassionate concern for the weak, the needy, and the helpless.

More than fifty years ago Robert A. Millikan said of science that it filled mankind with new vision and hope and striving for a better human existence, one that somewhat broadened human concern "from individual soul salvation to race salvation."[14] In a still earlier work he had observed that "by definitely introducing the most stimulating and inspiring motive for altruistic effort which has ever been introduced, namely the motive arising from the conviction that we ourselves may be the vital agents in the march of things, science has provided a reason for altruistic effort which is quite independent of the ultimate destination of the individual and is also much more alluring to some sorts of minds than singing hosannas forever around the throne."[15]

But as modern intellectuals have sought to find in this present world the religious values that earlier generations had found in the divine revelation of another world, moral principles have yielded to utility and expedience. The enormous potential of scientific technology, fusing theory and practice for unprecedented possibilities of control and change, has vastly maximized human possibilities not only for good, but also for evil. Nothing is more apparent in an age whose prized scientific methodology cannot identify objective values than its need for moral guidelines.

Whereas theistic scholars had patiently investigated the validity of ethical judgments, their present-day naturalistic successors replace such study of the *ought* by interest in the cultural history of moral concerns. Contemporary thought readily accommodates Feuerbach's notion that God is but man's own moral nature posited as absolute being, for a perpetually changing universe necessarily implies a changing humanity with changing ethics. The exaltation of inordinate self-interest at the expense of shared concern for humanity is a popular characteristic of modern life; not only Madison Avenue entrepreneurs but contemporary philosophers and clinical counselors defend and even advocate blatant egoism. The grim specter of a crumbling society poised for self-destruction has vanquished the once alluring vision of a scientific millennium. Self-centered moral philosophy disinterested in the character and purpose of the Creator-Redeemer God severs human beings from the dignity and worth of their true selfhood. Today's preoccupation with eros therefore has costly consequences for family and society.

To conjectural philosophers gifted with a special capacity for logical inconsistency, the thesis that human beings—even if chance byproducts of naturalistic evolution—should live by theistic principles of morality may seem strangely compelling. But for ordinary mortals, the atheistic denial of God and of eternal values and of a future life becomes an "open sesame" to selfishness and sensuality.

Inherent in the historically-given Word and Act of God is a creative moral power that philosophical speculation about human oughtness is powerless to impart. Among his covenant people the self-revealing Creator God nurtured compassion for the weak and helpless, concern for the destitute and needy, and solicitude for the stranger and outcast. A secular society may for a time shift to government the revealed responsibility of individuals, but an empirical perspective that mythologizes the existence of God will inevitably erode the foundations of biblical agape and default on its moral implications.

In the United States alone, abortion kills more than a million and a half fetuses annually. For contemporary society this issue perhaps more than any other distills the choice between yielding all sexual concerns either to hedonistic indulgence and its consequences, or to disciplined evaluation of human life and compassion for the weak and helpless.

Christianity does not measure human life simply by its functional value to society. Human worth is fixed by divine creation in the *imago Dei*, and Christ's redemptive death proclaims man's worth even in a sinful condition. Functional worth to society is therefore not the prime question about the survival of the genetically unwanted or disadvantaged, any more than private sexual pleasure, individual convenience, or the cultural mindset or totalitarian decree are to be considered the final determinant in evaluating fetal life.

Human life does not have infinite value, to be sure, for man is both a finite and contingent creature. Divine decree of the death penalty, which declares murder an affront to the divine image (Genesis 9:6), affirms at one and the same time that human life has immense worth *and* that this worth can be jeopardized. Whether the fetus is fully human prior to birth, and if so, whether its worth begins at conception, is a matter of ongoing debate. The contemporary secular view, which champions abortion on demand, differs totally from the Roman Catholic view which assigns the fetus full personhood from the very moment of conception. In the secular view the fetus is not truly human until the time of birth; its preservation or destruction is essentially only the mother's (or at most the parents') decision. The fact is that most abortions today are rationalized in terms of personal or pragmatic considerations; the mother's and/or mate's preference is the determining factor, and not some transcendent moral principle.

The biblical outlook indicts head-on all debate over survival of the fetus which reduces it to an issue of sexual pleasure or of private convenience, whether for physical or economic reasons. The scriptural view is that God gives life in the womb and that one dehumanizes sexual relationships by disjoining procreation and marriage and by treating intercourse as the mere momentary pleasure of two transitory partners.

What often complicate the issue of abortion are unfortunate pregnancies caused by incest or rape and fetuses subject to severe mental deformity. Seldom does birth of a baby any longer jeopardize the mother's survival; abortion is more frequently contemplated in reference to the mother's mental rather than physical condition. About 4 percent of all abortions occur at or beyond sixteen weeks of pregnancy and hence in the second trimester; it is generally assumed that of this 4 percent, at least 3 percent are performed because of severe life-depleting or life-threatening complications to either the fetus or the mother.

Where incest or rape is involved, one might argue for the legitimacy of abortion on the ground that God wills intercourse and conception within monogamous marriage, and that the aggrieved victim of assault should not in these circumstances be penalized by a violator's aggression. Authorities are often skeptical of a pregnancy attributed to rape, however, particularly if the indicated assault was not reported to police within 24 or 48 hours. Even here largely unexplored alternatives to abortion exist, including placement for adoption. When ecclesial agencies insist on preservation of fetal life under any and all circumstances, including that of severe physical deformities, should not such agencies be expected to share the otherwise crushing financial cost of sustaining such life?

Do therapeutic abortions differ in degrees of legitimacy? Where genetic deformity disallows mental and moral capacities identified with the *imago Dei*, does therapeutic abortion have greater justification than in cases of lesser deprivation? Some persons contend that the sanctity and dignity of full personhood belongs to every fetus—whatever its so-called quality—from the moment of conception, and that the biblical precedent of compassion towards the weak excludes abortion on any ground whatever. But even if therapeutic abortion should be allowable in cases of radical mental deformity, of incest and rape, and of actual threat to the mother's survival, no case could be made on moral grounds for destroying the at least 1,425,000 additional fetuses that comprise America's annual abortion statistics.

The passionate evangelical interest in the historical Jesus touches what is indispensable and central to genuine Christian belief. Apart from the fact of divine incarnation and Jesus Christ's sinlessness, substitutionary atonement, and bodily resurrection, the foundations of Christian faith collapse. Critical reconstructions of the role of Jesus betray, even require, an altered view of God. This is exemplified in David Friedrich Strauss's insistence that a thoroughly modern spirit must consider interest in the Jesus of history "anachronistic,"[16] as in Rudolph Bultmann's disavowal of it as based on a misunderstanding of Christianity,[17] and in Herbert Braun's view that the miraculous aspects of Jesus' life—from virgin birth to messiahship and ascension—merely attribute to the Nazarene legendary features borrowed from Hellenistic-oriental savior figures.[18]

Jesus bequeathed his followers no formal and schematic pattern of behavior. His messianic mission involved certain vocational commitments applicable only to him and to his own ministry. Nonetheless, he left an example of self-denial, of unreserved trust in and obedience to the Father, and of a life ever and fully open to the Holy Spirit that remains normative for Christians in all generations.

Yet we must not minimize the personal example of Jesus during his earthly ministry (as critics skeptical of biblical history are prone to do). Both liberation theology and the theology of revolution would profit, for example, from attending to the fact that neither Jesus nor the apostles he instructed promoted revolutionary liberation from Rome. Jesus' high view of sexual morality is another case in point. While modern relativists often demean it as simply a cultural reflex of Jewish heritage, they ignore the fact that the culture-conditionedness of ethics would also invalidate their own alternatives.

According to the New Testament, the Holy Spirit as an inner, renewable, divine resource is the wellspring of virtue and of the virtuous life. It would be hard to overstate the contrast of this view with that of the Greeks, especially Aristotle, and of the so-called "works religions" that connect salvation with human achievement rather than with divine grace. Aristotle taught that we attain the good life by harmoniously balancing our inner propensities by pursuing the "golden mean" that avoids extremes. But Christianity calls for death of the unregenerate nature and birth of a new nature by the Spirit of God, and not simply for a reshuffling of the old nature. In Jesus' words, "make a tree good and its fruit will be good" (Matthew 12:33).

Since the resurrection of the Crucified One, the ascended Christ in and by the Spirit has been personally present in believers as a dynamic, life-transforming power. Christian morality therefore has about it an element of buoyant Easter joy sustained by the Risen Jesus as our Eternal Contemporary. The regenerate believer does not live the Christian life autonomously "on his own," but he lives "in Christ" (Galatians 2:20) as one in whom Christ by the Spirit dwells and works. Christian morality is not merely conformity to a set of rules inferred from ethical principles, although the Risen Lord does in fact rule over the church in the world through the propositional teaching of the Bible; Christian morality participates also in the extension of divine sovereignty over the world through the Son's moral energizing of believers by the Spirit.

Whenever the New Testament speaks of the coming future restoration of the presently blemished divine image in man, it does so in terms of the believer's full conformity to the image of Jesus Christ (1 John 3:2, cf. Romans 8:29; Colossians 2:9). Where else in the history of human thought, we may ask, is the humanity God approves—both in earthly history and in eternity to come—so decisively and exclusively linked with the moral life and work of one person? While Jesus confidently confronted his foes with the question, "Can any of you prove me guilty of sin?" (John 8:46), those who knew him best attested his sinlessness.

Anyone who has pursued doctoral studies in theology and/ or philosophy knows how seldom the private life of founders of influential speculative systems and of great world religions is considered at all relevant, even when weighed by those systems or religions. Contemporary moralists write lengthy textbooks without a single reference to Jesus of Nazareth. Yet of whom can it be said as of the Nazarene that in him the Word truly became flesh? Earlier generations asked whether Socrates might perhaps have been saved on the ground of a positive response to general divine revelation. But most present-day scholarship in ethics is so largely out of touch with the gospels that it seldom asks the core question of the New Testament: Is Jesus of Nazareth God's one and only Son, or is he a deceiver, a blasphemer? And in the latter event, what would it say for the nature of things if the noblest impulses of all the centuries and the most immaculate life in history were the fruit of deception?

No emphasis finds profounder expression in Jesus' teaching than that on the kingdom of God. The Old Testament depicts God the Creator as King of the universe (Psalm 95:3-5) and regards the nations of this world (Psalm 22:8; Jeremiah 46:18) and their rulers (Daniel 2:37, 4:17, etc.) as under his jurisdiction. God is specially King of his covenant-people Israel (Deuteronomy 33:5; 1 Samuel 12:12) to whom he promised and gave their land. But when Israel's earthly kings disregarded him,

God punished them and sent the Hebrews into captivity. The inspired prophets had given assurance of a future era of peace and righteousness in which Messiah would succeed to David's throne. This messianic vision exerted an enduring influence upon Hebrew expectations.

During the interbiblical period, Jewish thought about the kingdom diversified into numerous strands, among them an emphasis on the individual's duty to submit to God's rule as stipulated by Mosaic law; nationalistic expectation of an earthly political kingdom which God would restore and over which God would rule while destroying Israel's oppressor nations; and anticipation that Messiah would, as God's agent, usher in a new era. Some writers more than others emphasized the kingdom's transcendent aspects above its earthly features. Others held out hope that the temple would be rebuilt, still others held that the righteous dead would be resurrected to share in the new age.

According to the Synoptic Gospels, what best summarizes the whole of Jesus' teaching is this theme of the kingdom or rule of God (Matthew 4:17; Mark 1:15; Luke 4:43). Jesus instructed his disciples to make it their main concern (Matthew 10:7; Luke 9:2).

Jesus focused not simply on God's transcendent eternal rule (Matthew 25:34f.), but also encouraged the view that his own earthly life and ministry constituted God's final redemptive act (Matthew 10:7; Luke 10:9f.) and that the eschatological kingdom had already dawned in his own conquest of sin, death, and Satan. He focused as well on a climactic future consummation when he, the Son of Man, would return in universal power and glory (Matthew 26:29). In the present interim, God anticipatively extends his kingdom rule as human beings participate individually in the kingdom through repentance and the new birth (John 3:3,5). Jesus' disciples constitute earth's new society; they are light and salt to the world, a regenerate *ecclesia* that the Risen Lord rules as living head of a body encompassing both believing Jews and Gentiles. His followers are to model a character and behavior exceeding that of Pharisees and scribes (Matthew 5:19f.). While not itself the kingdom, the church is the kingdom's most vital approximation and manifestation in the present age. Its ongoing mission is to extend the King's victory over the hostile forces of sin and evil, injustice and oppression; this it does by proclaiming the gospel, declaring and exemplifying the standards by which the King will judge mankind at his return, and witnessing to the present privileges and joys of serving the Risen Lord to whom all humanity must ultimately bow.

Jesus bids his disciples to pray daily (Matthew 6:10ff.) for the kingdom to come. Its future blessings go beyond its manifestation both in Jesus' historical life and ministry and in the new character and virtues bestowed daily by the Risen Lord through the Holy Spirit (Romans 14:17; Galatians 5:22). The Son of Man's second coming would be the occasion of the resurrection of the dead, the final judgment of humanity and of the nations, and the full conformity of all believers to the image of Jesus Christ.

This abbreviated reference to the kingdom of God will serve to illumine the impact of the Christian view of man in society upon subsequent Western thought. Until the present century it had been widely assumed, in view of biblical thought, that without divine regeneration sinful man could shape no historical utopia. Even Darwinians, although disdaining the doctrine of original sin, spoke guardedly of the perfectibility of man in view of supposed inherited brute impulses. But the biblical conviction of a final consummation of history in which good will surely prevail and evil is decisively conquered was metamorphosed into a secular doctrine of the kingdom, one unrelated to supernatural redemption and regeneration and linked instead to a supposed comprehensive law of evolutionary development. In the early part of our century an optimistic doctrine of the latent or essential goodness of man and of inevitable progress to utopia thus came to capture the speculative loyalty of scholars who had actually broken with biblical realities and vitalities, even while they mistakenly believed they had purified and elevated scriptural teaching.

It is remarkable how many modern social conceptualities are in fact secular reconstructions and mutations of biblical emphases. The communist notion of a future classless society in which the proletariat inherit the earth in a socialist utopia achieved by world revolution rests upon a perversion of basic biblical motifs. The transnational, transcultural, and transracial church provides a kind of picture of the League of Nations and then of the United Nations; these structures obscure rather than illumine revealed religion, however, and cloud God's transcendent purpose through the pluralistic nations to which the gospel is to be addressed. The modern vision of a warless world—in which nuclear energy is used only for peaceful purposes—has shallow roots in the biblical anticipation of an age when "swords will be beaten into plowshares" (Isaiah 2:4). Whatever its borrowed vocabulary or ideas, the modern view conspicuously suppresses the messianic component—that indispensable central ingredient of the biblical vision of the coming age of universal justice and peace.

With its dark view of human sin and of humanity's spiritual dilemma, the Bible assesses the moral compromises and the overweening self-interest of fallen human nature far more realistically than does the optimistic modern reading of man in society. The Bible recognizes the human need for a transformed character; it affirms the penitent sinner's access to redemptive reconciliation with God, and the genesis of a new nature in which God etches his law and will upon hearts dedicated to the love of God and his service; it finds the kingdom of God historically and anticipatively unveiled in the sinless life and resurrection of Messiah and reflected by the New Society over which Christ rules.

At the same time, world history falls within the universal providence of God as an arena in which the many nations serve as the context for both unregenerate and regenerate life, and in which civil government has a necessary though limited role. In this context, self-interest is not necessarily inordinate, but is one of the survival-promoting features of human existence. The misuse of power and freedom calls for public control, but public control is also one of the ways by which power is misused. The Christian conviction that flawed man is by nature selfish will alert him against the expectation that any economic or political system can be perfect. But the biblical outlook will also prevent him from viewing private property and wealth as inherently demonic, rather than as an entrustment for service of God and man. The Bible encourages labor for reward as well as for survival and insists upon fair wages; it approves private property, albeit not in terms of absolute right but rather of stewardship. It provides no basis for acclaiming a controlled economy as superior to a free market, as though bureaucracy is endowed with omnicompetence.

In summary, the moral fortunes of the West hinge both in the past and in the present upon the fate of the Bible and on appropriation or neglect of its spiritual and ethical realities. The sovereign, self-revealing, rational Creator is moving history toward a decisive moral denouement involving final judgment of both mankind and the nations. Speculative secular alternatives cannot vindicate objective morality and lead only to subjectivism and skepticism. The resources of revealed religion, including divine command morality which the messianic Redeemer fulfilled in the spirit of obedient love, together with the dynamic transforming power of the Holy Spirit, have in the past rescued the West from paganism and channeled agape at high tide into an otherwise bleak history.

The loss of biblical virtues and vitalities is the occasion of the moral confusion of our age, besieged as it now is by sensate, scientific, and sexual priorities. Its revered scientific method of knowing cannot identify fixed truth and the good. Only renewed respect for God's commandments can confront the cardinal vices of idolatry, murder, adultery, covetousness, and false witness that so conspicuously underlie modern social instability; and only renewed neighbor-love can defuse the many hostilities that plague community life. The Bible's pervasive regard for social justice enlivened by the bold witness of the prophets, its sure confidence in the invincibility of the dawning kingdom of

God, and its motivating and sustaining power for personal and public righteousness can, by the truth and vitalities of the gospel, bring to contemporary society the moral transformation it desperately needs.

"The God of the Bible and Moral Foundations," Notes

1. John Dewey, *A Common Faith* (New Haven, Conn.: Yale University Press, 1934).

2. Paul Kurtz, *The Fullness of Life* (New York: Horizon Press, 1974), 16.

3. Emil Brunner, *Christianity and Civilization* (London: Nisbet, 1948), 18.

4. Arthur F. Holmes, *Contours of a World View* (Grand Rapids: Wm. B. Eerdmans Publishing Co., 1983), 7.

5. Nahum Sarna, "Understanding Creation in Genesis," in *Is God a Creationist?*, ed. by Roland Mushat Frye (New York: Charles Scribner's Sons, 1983), 168f.

6. *Euthyphro*, 9e.

7. Martin Luther, *The Bondage of the Will*, Chap. 5, Sec. VI.

8. Jeffrey Stout, *The Flight from Authority* (Notre Dame, Ind.: University of Notre Dame Press, 1981), ix.

9. G.E.M. Anscombe, "Modern Moral Philosophy," *Philosophy* 33 (January 1958): 1-19.

10. Janine Marie Idziak, *Divine Command Morality: Historical and Contemporary Readings* (New York: The Edwin Mellon Press, 1979).

11. Eric Voegelin, *Israel and Revelation* (Baton Rouge: Louisiana State University Press, 1956), 113, 315f.

12. John Jefferson Davis, *Foundations of Evangelical Theology* (Grand Rapids: Baker Book House, 1984), 253.

13. Anders Nygren, *Agape and Eros* (London: S.P.C.K., 1963), 2:39.

14. Robert A. Millikan, *Science and the New Civilization* (New York: Charles Scribner's Sons, 1931), 78.

15. Robert A. Millikan, *Evolution in Science and Religion* (New Haven: New York University Press, 1927), 83f.

16. David Friedrich Strauss, *The Christ of Faith and the Jesus of History*, 1965.

17. Rudolph Bultmann, *Jesus Christ and Mythology* (New York: Charles Scribner's Sons, 1958).

18. Herbert Braun, *Jesus of Nazareth: The Man and His Time*, trans. Everett R. Kalin (Philadelphia: Fortress Press, 1979), 25.

Twenty Fantasies of a Secular Society

A mong the fantasies embraced by our secular society, the following stand out as especially alluring and potentially destructive:

1. That democracy is secure as long as individual rights are stressed.

Without shared values, democracy is on the move to anarchy. The notion that the strength of democracy lies solely in its tolerance of diversity distorts the principle that a nation's feeling for justice is reflected by its attitude toward minorities. The prevalent notion that uncritical tolerance of all deviation is intrinsic to democracy forfeits to totalitarian bureaucracies all interest in absolutes; the state then imposes social imperatives merely as its own omnipotent will. America's founding fathers considered religion and morality the twin supports of a democracy; they did not champion a state that defames religion or creatively defines morality. Secular humanists frequently plead pluralism to advance positions that are pointedly antitheistic and that consolidate the prejudices of a deviate minority. But

A presentation at Shavano Institute for National Leadership in Colorado, 21 May 1984.

responsibility to God undergirds responsibility to society and best reinforces human rights.

2. *That natural factors govern the course of history and that political wisdom best guarantees national survival.*

However astute its leaders, no nation has an advance guarantee of perpetuity if it trades moral absolutes for so-called political prudence. Only God assuredly knows the future, even the future of the nations, and he frequently punishes rebellious nations with mediocre leadership.

3. *That God relates himself to humans only as a God of love, and that he will protect the United States and its people from catastrophic disaster because of our commitment to freedom, generosity, and goodness.*

Most Americans vote for God despite the atheistic head winds of the twentieth century. But for many, God is an ever-living George Washington who serves invisibly as the father of our country. This vague political theology assumes that America can never drift irrecoverably beyond divine approval, and that the nation is intrinsically exempt from severe and final divine judgment.

4. *That the American people are essentially good at heart in a world whose inhabitants are more prone to evil.*

Vast reserves of spiritual and moral power remain in lands which, like America, have been enlightened by Christianity and where evangelical ideals remain to motivate even a secular society that does not wholly live by the Bible, yet responds benevolently to world need. But shall we call a nation "good" if most of its unwed teenagers indulge in premarital intercourse, if it has a million or more abortions each year, if it has a 40 percent divorce rate and an epidemic of venereal disease? Would we call another nation "good" if its mass media push to the outer margins of public debate those who speak the biblical mind and call for a character-transforming alternative? Would we call another nation "good" if an educational elite eroded from schoolroom textbooks any teaching about the living God of the Bible, and about the Ten Commandments and the Sermon on the Mount, and censored the doctrines of divine creation and divine redemption and divine judgment?

Does not America need an antidefamation network to challenge those who vilify champions of public morality as prolongers of the Inquisition and as "book burners," when in fact humanists discriminate against *Christian* reading and conservative evangelicals read as many books as any other segment of the population? So-called guardians of freedom invoke democracy, tolerance, and openmindedness to spend public funds for sexually permissive library reading. Why must parents be considered pernicious when they demand that sex education courses for teenagers convey not only Morton Hunt's effusive claim that "nearly all young men and four-fifths of young women have sexual intercourse before they marry" (*The Young Person's Guide to Love*, p. 59), but also the sober biblical emphasis that non-intercourse before marriage is not an archaic notion that aims to deprive young people of legitimate pleasure, but is a moral commitment that delights the heart of God?

5. *That capitalism's inherent superiority as an economic system guarantees its survival, irrespective of moral and spiritual commitments.*

It is true that a free market economy has built-in balances between self-interest and social-interest, since manufacturers or workers who provide ineffective products or services sooner or later discourage a demand for their output. Get-rich-quick shysters barely operating within the law can no doubt move hurriedly from one lucrative scheme to another, and major corporations can mount lobbies to protect their special interests. But a free society provides opportunity to revise the law, and the exposure of inordinate self-interest sooner or later becomes a free market liability. Only a divine reinforcement and renewal of ethical imperatives provides adequate moral restraints in any society, because fallen human nature caters to self-interest more readily than to moral imperatives.

6. *That capitalism is supportive of Christianity while Marxism is destructive of it.*

While Marxist countries have for various reasons impeded and opposed Christian activity, secular capitalism can also erode the Judeo-Christian heritage. Large corporations have frequently funded causes engaged in revolutionary social change. When big business promotes its products by trivializing for commercial purposes the spiritual and cultural heritage of the West (e.g., Baskin-Robbins's use of Handel's *Messiah* as background music to laud its "heavenly" ice cream), it indirectly weakens the Judeo- Christian inheritance. When the CBS network uses the "Hallelujah Chorus" to close out coverage of U.S. victories at the Pan-American Games, it not only betrays a lack of reverence but also serves to paganize the religious heritage of the West. The salvation God provides in Christ has nothing in common with athletic prowess. The use of Scripture references with a double entendre in cinema and theater frequently degrades into a crude joke, and sometimes into a carnal banter, what spiritually sensitive generations have prized as a sacred treasure.

7. *That poverty is the worst social evil, one that governmental action can and must promptly and universally eliminate.*

The vision of a present world-order without poverty was not present in Old Testament thought, or in ancient Graeco-Roman thought, or in New Testament thought, or in medieval Christian thought. The Bible teaches that God has a special eye for the destitute and that those who are entrusted with more than their needy neighbors have a duty to be compassionate. This duty is universal and devolves on non-Christians as well as Christians. But the Bible does not teach a forced redistribution of wealth.

8. *That capitalist economics is to blame for the existence and predicament of the poor.*

The "poor" existed long before capitalist economics, which is often blamed for their existence, and Marxism has not eliminated an impoverished class. The worst impoverishment of mankind is well-nigh universal in view of the spiritual and moral rebellion of the human race. The Marxist state worsens this plight by a suppression of public freedom.

9. *That any alternative to secular Western culture would be superior, and that a communist society has virtues that make it attractive to a sensitive spirit.*

In *The Betrayal of the West* Jacques Ellul says: "Look back over the films of the last 20 years, and you will see to your amazement that the only successful ones have been those that have broadcast scorn for the West, filth, and self-scourging" (p. 149). Ellul writes of the "unqualified negation of all the West has been and can yet be. . . . Everything of a positive character that may be found is immediately turned inside out, distorted, and stood on its head." At the same time, Marxism is lauded as altruistic and the communist record is obscured—including its predatory military expansion, the Soviet gulag, its repression of dissent, its compromises of religious liberty, and blatant discrimination in university faculties against any and all critics of atheism. Meanwhile, the West is deplored for its arsenal of military defenses and is blamed for promoting global instability.

10. *That only radical alarmists consider modern culture worse than cultures of the past.*

There is no need to glamorize the past. Toynbee reminds us that every great civilization has ended in rubble and ruin, and the study of history makes clear that every great world power has sooner or later become second-rate, and some have glided off the map entirely. No culture can survive in the absence of shared beliefs and values. Past civilizations have crumbled when social cohesion has vanished, and the modern nations are currently in deep trouble. Ours is the first generation in history to attempt to build a culture on naturalistic relativism. Those who say that one culture is as good as another usually hold a relativistic view of values and cannot objectively identify any society as better or worse than another. Modern culture can be graded better or worse only if there are fixed standards. God knows what will survive his searching judgment, and it is likely to be less than what we nominate for divine applause. God sometimes spares an ungodly culture for the sake of a godly minority, but when a rebellious society caricatures and vilifies its godly minority and ridicules fixed values and divine truth, it invites divine judgment.

11. *That the value of human life is most pointedly signaled by anguished concern over a possible nuclear holocaust.*

But if protest is simultaneously muted over the millions of abortions that modern nations routinely accommodate, such selective morality presumptively cloaks itself as a comprehensive concern for social righteousness when it is nothing of the sort. There is no moral virtue in selective murder. The fact that Hitler preserved Aryans does not excuse his destruction of millions of others.

12. *That personal earthly survival is the supreme value to which all other concerns should be subordinated.*

The philosophy that "nothing is worth dying for" accommodates the most ruthless barbarism and the most abject slavery. In his latest book, *Marxism and Beyond*, even the humanist Sidney Hook comments pointedly that "Those who say life is worth living at any cost have already written for themselves an epitaph of infamy, for there is no cause and no person they will not betray to stay alive." This philosophy produces young Americans who will not even register for any possibility of future military draft, even while a smiling but misguided Iranian on a suicide mission drives his explosives-laden van into the Beirut compound of a peace-keeping mission.

13. *That science is our salvation, for it enables us to control the forces of nature and to shape our destiny.*

Science has indeed expanded human convenience and comfort. But it has not made man wiser, better, or happier. The empirical method of knowing cannot illumine the supernatural world, cope with the moral realities of good and evil, or contend with the dilemmas of death and destiny. Science cannot even foresee the devastating ramifications of its own scientific achievements.

14. *That science is to be specially treasured because of the moral permissiveness it accommodates.*

The scientific method has no competence to decide moral issues. It enables modern lovers to escape the physical consequences of sex, rewards steroid-doping athletes with international medals and lucrative contracts, and shapes other possibilities of evading ethical concerns. Yet scientists, no less than others, are responsible to the moral law and should not be mute about ethical implications of the uses to which their discoveries are put.

15. *That the mass media's prime role is to reflect contemporary personal and social values.*

An institution concerned mainly to dramatize the agonies and dilemmas of modern society and to mirror its vices has little awareness of a blighted civilization waiting to be plowed under by its own delinquency. It becomes increasingly difficult to make a dignified appeal for decency while the media make capital of a generation whose values are scrambled and skewed, whose deepest impulses are sexual and monetary, whose sexual madness is marked by fast-fading intimacies. Even magazines that once were family-oriented, like *Redbook*, have become sexually explicit. Some large-circulation daily newspapers periodically run features that imitate *Playboy*. An elitist view, one that condones an ethics of convenience and regards biblical imperatives as less legitimate than secular preferences, dismisses those who question the ultimate value of such programs as promoting censorship.

But no institution can be exonerated for ignoring the unrecognized dangers of a deceptive culture if it tunes out as "uninteresting social criticism" that which does not garb itself in spicy comments on current sexual mores, even while its reportorial gossips generously discuss the exotic features and sordid orgies of our age. A balanced media would counter-question the moral insurgents who would sweep our lives clean of traditional virtues; it would challenge those who have produced a contemporary clan so confused about good and evil that they consider such distinctions to be merely statements about our personal feelings, and who debunk as emotionally-based propaganda the views of those who would preserve objective norms of societal decency.

16. *That serious literature, including philosophy, ethical, and scientific theory, concerns only the intellectual elite; its neglect by the masses should not disturb us.*

Degeneration of interest in the formative intellectual theories can only yield dire results. Not simply does this neglect accommodate a society that finds its priority in sensory stimulus and gratification, but it also ignores the basic issues of the meaning of human history and life and of the worth of man. Ideas have immense implications for good or evil. Neither a universe ruled by change nor one ruled by mechanical determinism allows room for right and wrong, moral duty and decision, or for obeying one's conscience and living by moral conviction. Neither in nature, nor in society, nor even in tradition as such, can man find an absolute norm that unconditionally obliges him. A generation of scientific genius cannot tell us what is good or evil; yet it can initiate a chain reaction of genetic mutation that could ruin mankind and perhaps all other life forms, litter the environment with unforeseen nuclear waste, and perhaps even loft the earth itself, fragmented by a nuclear blast, into outer space. The French materialists who declared that Christianity was dead and that science would precipitate an earthly paradise never dreamed how devastating might be the applications of science by men who abolished the commandments of God.

17. *That one gets a liberal education if all learning is molded by atheistic assumptions.*

There is a vast accumulation of Hebrew and Christian learning without which secular modern scholarship impoverishes itself. In the absence of an intellectual vision of God and of fixed ethical imperatives, modern learning is left with inconsistent and often incoherent commitments. Emphasis merely on value-clarification indicates the conflicting value-claims of a pluralistic society, but it cannot establish authentic values. It places man at the center of the cosmos while it insists that man himself is evolving in an expanding universe—and it abandons stable standards of right and wrong. A civilization with no firm intellectual core, searching for the meaning of modern experience while it forsakes transcendent and abiding meaning, engages in a vain quest for true understanding. The danger to social stability today is posed not by a "mindless orthodoxy" but by dogmatic deviancy from final truth and eternal moral norms. The cognitive blackout of eternal truth and of a fixed good bankrupts the realm of ideas and values, and restricts human knowledge to revisable perceptions of the changing world of nature.

18. *That Judeo-Christian beliefs and values are pertinent only to the private outlook of a specially religious segment of society, and do not illumine the present culture-crisis or bear decisively on its outcome.*

The present collapse of Western learning into philosophical skepticism and moral relativism results from the attempt of the Enlightenment to expound religion, law, ethics, history, literature, and the arts apart from the self-revealing God of biblical theism; God, the Enlightenment said, is irrelevant to the intellectual debate. But the loss of Judeo-Christian heritage has in fact led to the modern forfeiture of fixed moral principles and of final truth. The incohesion of contemporary learning, its lack of cognitive unity and of integrative power, result from the forfeiture of biblically-given criteria for the understanding of nature, man, history, and transcendent realities. The brilliant insights of modern learning have not identified the character of ultimate reality, and its concentrated focus on anthropology leaves scholars unsure about the essential nature and destiny of man. Under these circumstances, how can the study of history yield a consensus about the course and meaning of human events? It is time to refocus the options, to identify the prejudices that set modern thought on its antibiblical course, and to reinvestigate the cohesive intellectual alternative that Judeo-Christian theism offers.

19. *That public discussion of metaphysical concerns and ethical absolutes is nationally confusing and in a pluralistic society is unnecessarily divisive.*

In these circumstances what we have in common reduces to nature, money, and sex—priorities that become seductive because all other concerns are privatized. In earlier generations

Americans, despite their cultural diversity, shared a certain theistic and moral consensus. The loss of God and the eternal good, of revealed truths and fixed principles, gives right-of-way to evolutionary conceptions and hence to commitments that change with shifting patterns of culture reshaped from generation to generation, based entirely on sociological conditions. Nature, history, and even society may therefore be manipulated for whatever objectives man is able to impose upon his environment.

20. *That it makes little difference to the modern world whether belief in God becomes publicly significant in American life.*

It is not enough that some Americans see the face of God and strive to do his will and to honor him; whether government is above God, whether public institutions conduct their affairs as if God were nonexistent or irrelevant, that will decide the future of the free world. No atheistic option can consistently avoid relativizing morality and brutalizing man. One reason American foreign policy falters is that our leaders fail to see that differences between modern nations are largely rooted in religion. We as the leading world power cheapen our religious heritage, and the Soviet Union seeks its destruction. But God remains a mightier power than all the military might of all the modern nations. Wolfhart Pannenberg remarks: "The almighty freedom to do constantly new, previously unheard-of things is characteristic of the God of the Old Testament. Jeremiah expressed this as a word of Yahweh himself: 'Behold, I am the LORD, the God of all flesh; is anything too hard for me?' (Jeremiah 32:27)" (*What is Man?*, p. 144).

The linkage of God's sovereignty with all flesh concerns not only man's origins and resurrection destiny, but also the fearsome crossroads of contemporary international violence. The apostle Paul expressly characterized God as the one "who gives life to the dead and calls things that are not as though they were" (Romans 4:17).

Nothing to Worry About?

*I*t was some forty years ago, but I remember it well: a baby's cry at three in the morning. I reached out my hand, rocked the carriage, and groggily assured our firstborn that his daddy was near and that all was well: "Sleep, baby, sleep . . . . Don't worry about a thing!"

I recalled this nightly exercise the other day when I read the Sermon on the Mount and noted again how, almost repetitiously, Jesus exhorted his disciples: "Do not worry" (Matthew 6:25,31,34), "Why do you worry?" (6:28).

At the beginning of the twentieth century, many theologians and philosophers also were saying "there's nothing to worry about." They said it, however, on foolhardy assumptions, like that of the essential goodness of man, the inevitability of progress, and utopia-just-around-the-corner. Swiss theologian Karl Barth also preached that optimistic view until he was suddenly shocked awake. The steady loss of young men from his congregation and the ever-increasing black armbands worn by women whose husbands and sons and sweethearts would

Sermon at St. Peter's Episcopal Church, Hillsdale, Michigan, 26 February 1984, at the baptism of Jacob Stewart Roche.

never return from the battlefields of World War I shattered his confidence in the future. Barth then read and reread Paul's Epistle to the Romans. There he found plenty to worry about: the sinfulness of man, the perversity of history, the dread judgment of a holy God, man's need of supernatural salvation.

Some years ago while lecturing abroad, I lodged with a professor friend in Seoul, Korea. One Sunday morning as he left very early to preach at an army compound, he said, "Don't worry about a thing!" Soon I heard strange noises in that unfamiliar home and on investigating found that water pipes in the basement were leaking—in fact, leaking furiously. Mrs. Henry and I set to work at once emptying pans and then pails of water as we tried to cope with a situation that worsened steadily, for in that maze of pipes I could not find the master control. "Don't worry . . . don't worry about a thing" is scant comfort when one is caught in a swirl of circumstances that seemingly have no purpose and are indifferent to personal concerns.

It is that way, too, when modern scientism postulates a universe without purpose, regards man as an accidental by-product of an evolutionary explosion, and engulfs human personality in a network of impersonal processes. Someone has called this an effort to capture the real world in a laboratory test tube. It leads to the contemporary creed, "I believe in Big Bang yesterday, in Big Brother or Big Bucks today, and in Big Blank in the life to come." Adept at controlling cosmic power, scientism is a stranger to moral and spiritual power. Once hailed as the biggest advance in Western civilization, the atomic age now cannot cope with nuclear waste and even trembles as the clock of destiny ticks, perhaps relentlessly, toward nuclear midnight.

"Sleep, baby, sleep! Don't worry about a thing!" No, Jacob Stewart Roche, there is much to worry about; there is good reason to cry in the night. The prophets of liberty are vanishing, and freedom is fragile and not self-sustaining. Predatory powers are restless for world revolution. Totalitarian nations have gulags. And free world nations mortgage their future by spiritual neglect.

Sooner than you know, Jacob Stewart, you may need to decide whether some ideals are worth living for, even worth dying for. You will need to decide whether to betray or to augment the great moral and spiritual heritage of the West. Someday you must decide between deities true and deities false, and choice of the wrong God will lead to a dead end for human worth and destiny. We refuse to yield you to a world of chance and change and relativism and skepticism; we who cherish you, claim you instead for the living Lord, for God the Creator and Redeemer and Judge.

When Jesus said, "Do not worry," he knew only too well the horrendous reality of evil and the dread depth of the human predicament. He knew the whole range of earthly anxieties: "The pagans run after these things" (Matthew 6:32), he said, the things they made their priorities—food, raiment, survival.

But when Jesus said, "Do not worry," he was reassuring disciples and believers, not pagans. Put first the kingdom of God and his righteousness he said, and everything else will fall into place. "Do not worry."

His point was not that natural evils and moral evils do not exist, or that believers will be spared hardship and pain and suffering. In Jesus' day, anesthesia and antibiotics were unknown; pain was unmitigated pain, and suffering was unmitigated suffering. Saul of Tarsus wrote, moreover, that the apostles were perceived as "men condemned to die . . . a spectacle to the whole universe . . . fools for Christ . . . the scum of the earth" (1 Corinthians 4:9f.). He suffered political injustice, and at the height of his career was confined to the Mamertine prison. When you are in Rome, see for yourself what sort of hellhole it was.

What Jesus taught his disciples was to put God first and to subsume all else under him—*everything*: Caesar, survival, money, status, power, everything. Caesar has his place, but there is one Lord, the Lord Jesus Christ; survival has its place, but he that clings to physical life above all other values betrays eternal perspectives; mammon has its place, but love of money is a root of evil; other things have their place as well, but life's true fullness does not consist of an infinity of sex, of status, or of things.

Accordingly, the early Christians anchored their lives to three great certainties:

(1) They knew that—for the believer—the worst that can happen is already past. God had already judged their sin and Christ had borne it; they had made their own the redemption that is in Christ Jesus. They knew Jesus as "the way to the Father."

(2) They knew that—for the believer—however dark it may be, the present always has a brighter side. "And we know that in all things God works for the good of those who love him, who have been called according to his purpose" (Romans 8:28). For Paul, the "all things" of Romans 8:28 included even "the things that happened" to him in Rome (Philippians 1:12), including his imprisonment and eventual execution by Roman soldiers. As the psalmist put it: "He alone is my rock and my salvation; he is my fortress . . . trust in him at all times" (Psalm 62:6f.). God is the God of all seasons and the God of "all things."

(3) They knew that—for the believer—the best that will happen lies in the future. Even sudden death is sudden glory, for to be "with Christ" is "better," yea, "far better" than what this earthly life offers.

When Jesus impressed these truths on his disciples he was poised on the very brink of eternity. It was while on the way to the cross, to his own crucifixion, that he told his disciples to believe in God and also in him, the Redeemer Son. On the way to the cross it was Jesus who had peace, whereas the disciples, although not facing crucifixion, had troubled hearts. To those troubled disciples and to us as well Jesus bequeathed his own unique peace: "Peace I leave with you; my peace I give you. I do not give to you as the world gives." (John 14:27).

I tell you that a peace that can look beyond the terrors of crucifixion to resurrection morning—yea, a peace that can see in the very death on the cross itself God's victory over all that would put an end to Christ's cause, and the conquest of death itself—is a peace adequate for any exigency that you or I will ever be called upon to face. On that cross, divine mercy triumphed; by the Suffering Servant our debt was paid.

Abba, Father—literally in Aramaic, *Daddy*—has his eye on the cradle of his children. When we cry in the night, a nail-pierced hand beckons us not to worry. "My peace I give you," said Jesus. "Do not let your hearts be troubled and do not be afraid." "Why do you worry?"

On Being beside Yourself

> And when [those who were near him] heard it, they
> went out to seize him, for people were saying "He is
> beside himself" (Mark 3:21, RSV).

*A*t some point in life, if statisticians are right, one in ten
Americans has a breakdown. So stressful is modern living
that almost everyone has a mother or a father, a sister or a
brother, or some other relative, who has suffered psychological
disorder.

In times of physical crisis we can usually find some way to
help. But seldom do we feel so incapable of helping than when
a loved one has a mental breakdown. No pastoral problem is
more difficult, a pastor-friend of mine recently confided, than
helping a church family cope with the problem of a loved one
who has suddenly lost his or her mind.

I have no personal contact with the Hinckley family, but
when news about the assassination attempt on President Reagan
reached their home in Colorado, I suspect the family's immediate reaction was that John Jr. must have gone out of his
mind. What spontaneous response would the parents have had
to the shock waves of the national news—active as they were in
a neighborhood Bible study, the father sometimes volunteering

---

A sermon preached on Mark 3:7-35 at Duke University chapel on 21 March
1982.

as a World Vision consultant—other than to think that their son had suddenly gone mad.

On one occasion the acquaintances of Jesus thought he showed signs of a mental breakdown and was desperately in need of help. You remember that Jesus had left the carpentry shop and began preaching; crowds gathered as he worked miracles and then called for disciples. Some of his townspeople said he was "beside himself." Those who knew Jesus most intimately decided it would be best to take Jesus and to isolate him.

We're not sure whether those who went to seize Jesus were his immediate family including Mary and Jesus' brothers, or other close relatives, or friends of the family. The Greek text says only that "those with him . . . went out to seize him."

We're not even sure what motivated them to take Jesus away. We would like to think that love and concern for Jesus prompted their action in the face of an ugly and disconcerting rumor: "They said," the text reads, " 'He is beside himself.' "

Who are the anonymous *they*? Were they townspeople in the crowd who knew Jesus only as the carpenter of Nazareth? Or were they, more specifically, the theologians, that is, the scribes who in context declare that Jesus is possessed by a demon?

The human mind, in any event, is very fragile; it sometimes gives way even in the godliest of families. And what can more grievously choke the spirit than to hear neighbors or townspeople rumoring that one of the family no longer knows what he's doing, that he is mentally over the brink and has gone berserk. He's "beside himself."

Not long ago an aged widow, long active in a Canadian church, mentally snapped. A police car took her captive at a main highway crossroads. There she was, furiously directing traffic in competition with the automatic signals; automobiles and their frustrated drivers were backed up for blocks. She could have been your mother or mine. She didn't know what she was doing: she was "beside herself."

I first met people living in this twilight zone when I was a teenager. Our large family moved from New York City to a one-acre Long Island plot that my father could buy only because the price was right. One reason the price was right was its location not far from what was then the world's largest state hospital for the insane. Our house was in the escape corridor. As a lad of fifteen I worked as a summer attendant in a therapeutic ward monitoring those strange human beings who were beside themselves. A half century later I still vividly recall human hulks struggling to make a recovery by pushing floor polishers or by weaving and sewing hour after hour and day after day in search of order in their disordered lives. The first university graduate I ever knew was a patient who escaped from that confinement only to be reconfined, a Yale alumnus ravaged by alcohol and debilitated to institutional commitment before he was thirty. He had delirium tremens; he was "beside himself."

Our response to loved ones who act strangely is often prejudiced by self-interest as much as it is motivated by the victim's sorry condition; we feel threatened or vulnerably exposed because someone close to home is in trouble. There's reason to think that alongside whatever deep concern they felt for Jesus, the brothers of Jesus (and perhaps Mary also) may have chafed under great personal embarrassment.

We know on the basis of later testimony, even by Jesus' brethren, that Jesus was not in fact out of his mind despite what unbelieving scribes or theologians were saying, and despite what even some of the family may have thought at the time. The context illumines the quite natural feelings of Jesus' kinsmen. Jesus, after all, had begun speaking about a "new family"—not a natural family of blood ties, but a spiritual family. Picture the scene: after unbelieving religionists declared Jesus possessed by an unclean spirit, Jesus' mother and brothers arrive to take Jesus away. As Mark relates it, "a crowd was sitting round him, and they told him, 'Your mother and brothers are outside looking for you.'" Jesus' reply shocked them: "'Who are my mother and my brothers?' he asked. Then he looked at those seated in a circle around him and said, 'Here are my mother and my brothers! Whoever does God's will is my brother, and sister, and mother'" (Mark 3:31-35).

So it was that while Mary and his brethren waited to take him home Jesus spoke emphatically about the "new family." They had come to shield Jesus whom the religious leaders had already declared demon-possessed. Could anything have been more embarrassing, therefore, than to hear Jesus speak publicly of another family than his own, of deeper ties to a different family—to a family, as we would put it, supernational, superracial, supercultural?

To say Jesus is "beside himself" can in fact be a desperate but convenient way of hiding the embarrassment we feel in his presence and of defensively transferring to him our own moral nakedness and mental disarrangement. It isn't Jesus, it is we who tend to be beside ourselves, to be mindless of true spiritual realities. We profess to be the family of Jesus, presuming to have a special claim on him, eager to take him home. But here he is: talking publicly about family in a way that embarrasses us. He exposes our vulnerabilities and reveals our compromises. He unmasks our prejudices—spiritual prejudices, racial prejudices, national prejudices, and cultural prejudices. Jews considered Gentiles a cut lower than God's chosen humanity; Hitler considered Jews a cut lower than Aryans; white Christians sometimes even today find it hard, if not offensive, to speak of a black brother or black sister in God's intimate family.

Our religious neutrality is threatened whenever someone we know well takes spiritual commitment seriously and refuses any longer to play hide-and-seek and touch-and-go with the living God. Jesus knew the damaging effects of self-serving religion. He made public the faults of Pharisees and Sadducees in his day and even now challenges our self-seeking commitments. In the sixties, thousands of respectable American churchgoers were upset when sons or daughters embraced the Jesus movement and emerged with a new scale of values, a new regard for the Bible, and a new awareness of what it means to be a Christian. "He's just like those Jesus-people," said a neighbor of mine about a son at college who had joined the ranks; "Why," his mother added apprehensively, "he's even praying for us."

What easier cover is there for one's own indifference than to label another's spiritual aggressiveness as a kind of fanatical enthusiasm? The family wanted to take Jesus home, not simply out of concern for Jesus, but because the family wished to escape public embarrassment.

To an unregenerate world, not only will Jesus seem out of step with reality, but so will his disciples. Think and act like the world and the world will embrace us, for then being a Christian doesn't make a speck of difference. But truly live in the Spirit world as did early Christians and worldlings will consider us zombies—over the brink and stark mad.

The scribes of today are still prone to move spiritual ultimates to the margins of stable personhood. Many psychology texts now mention God only when referring to religious aberrations; that tells more about secular prejudices than about spiritual realities. Atheistic rulers go a step farther: they allow no public role whatever for religious conscience. Some even turn mental hospitals from humane institutions into centers for suppressing political dissent, and they condemn champions of religious freedom and other critics of the system to psychiatric wards.

Jesus put the matter sharp and clear: this world, he said, hates the people of God. "If the world hates you," said Jesus, "know that it has hated me before it hated you. If you were of the world, the world would love its own; but because you are not of the world, but I chose you out of the world, therefore the world hates you" (John 15:18-19, RSV). Never did he declare the danger of being in league with false assumptions more emphatically than when he warned: "the hour is coming when whoever kills you will think he is offering service to God" (John 16:2, RSV).

The early Christians weren't much surprised therefore when the worldly-wise despised them as fools and called their preaching foolishness. "We are fools [*moros*]," writes the apostle Paul (1 Corinthians 4:10)—absurd and idiotic, embarked on a wrong course, and doing mad things—"fools," he adds, "for Christ." He then invites those who revel in their worldly wisdom to hear what seemingly foolish outrages he has gladly endured so that others might hear the truth of the gospel: imprisonment, beatings, lashings, stoning, shipwreck, dangers, hunger, thirst, and exposure, all for the sake of Christ (2 Corinthians 11:16ff.). Every true Christian shares in this derision, even if only in elemental ways that seem trivial alongside Paul's sufferings for Christ. In my early newspaper days, after I became a Christian, a fellow reporter quite regularly introduced me to visiting dignitaries as "our 'God-man.'" Today's student cynics heap the same ridicule upon the campus God-squad, and humanists consider a "christer" unbearable.

The New Testament calls for a new selfhood and a new set of values; it seeks transformation of the mind no less than transformation of the will. It speaks of unsettled minds, divided minds, misguided minds, distorted minds, hardened minds, corrupt minds—a rather intimidating list of adjectives. "A double-minded man," writes James, brother of the Lord, "is unstable in all he does . . . That man should not think he will receive anything from the Lord" (James 1:7f.).

To be sure, the problem of becoming a Christian is not that the truth about God cannot be intellectually cognized and universally known. Nor are the laws of logic in dispute. Christianity stresses that all human beings are sinners; this emphasis presupposes that all mankind shares the light of God's general revelation and shamefully revolts against it.

It is to "those who are perishing," says Paul, that "the message of the cross is foolishness" (1 Corinthians 1:18). But to the humble and penitent, God gives a share in divine wisdom. "I will put my laws in their minds" (Hebrews 8:10), said the God of covenant; "I will write them on their minds" (Hebrews 10:16). Paul calls for renewing of the mind (Romans 12:2). "Set your mind on God's kingdom" (Matthew 6:33, NEB), said Jesus.

During those long nights in prayer that Jesus spent alone with the Father, away from the spiritual myopia of his contemporaries, did planet Earth perhaps seem to Jesus like a vast mental institution—a runaway world of humans all but out of their right mind? Just as multitudes in mental hospitals appear to medics and nurses like mankind beside itself, does our renegade humanity sometimes strike God as virtually disordered and deranged? Whether God revealed himself in general revelation or in special revelation, man in sin preferred darkness to light. "Although they knew God," Paul writes of the Gentiles, "their thinking became futile and their foolish hearts were darkened. Although they claimed to be wise, they became fools" (Romans 1:21f.). The Jews compounded this rebellion by disavowing Messiah; as a classic text in John's Gospel tells us, the Logos of God "came to that which was his own, but his own did not receive him" (John 1:11).

Among the placard carriers who trudge the streets of New York, occasionally one still finds a lonely purveyor of wisdom who gets us coming and going. Coming toward us his message reads: A FOOL FOR CHRIST; seen from behind, its corollary question asks: WHOSE FOOL ARE YOU?

Modern relativists dismiss this extravaganza as the vestige, the remnant of a long outdated past. By a single stroke their naturalistic dogma declares not only the claims of Christ but any proclamation of final truth and moral absolutes to be foolish. The current tolerance of moral indecency takes refuge in the indulgent spirit of democracy and classifies absolutes with the ugly mentality of totalitarian dictatorships. For naturalism, all ideas and ideals are culture-bound; it declares every system of philosophy and morality, every religion as well, relative to its historical environment and subject to inevitable revision. It bans to the realm of myth the Judeo-Christian insistence on supernatural revelation, divine commandments, fixed truths, and ethical absolutes. In the New Testament the naturalistic mentality discovers not an agenda of enduring spiritual and moral values, but an unacceptable intolerance, one that breeds a society unable to accept the validity of conflicting truth-claims.

An affable, secular humanism champions social imperatives like concern for the needy, love for neighbor, justice for the oppressed, and ecological sensitivity.

All these ideals are borrowed fragments of biblical beliefs

shorn of any firm metaphysical standing by a naturalistic outlook that reduces reality to impersonal processes and events. If
all realms of being are temporal and contingent, if truth and the
good are culture-relative, if man is himself the autonomous
source of right and wrong, humanism too is on the auction
block, despite the refusal of humanism to apply to itself the demands of relativity that it forces on all other perspectives. Push
its preferred dogmas as it will, humanism cannot manipulate the
history of thought by entrenching its prejudices at the pinnacle
of the world of ideas. Recent philosophy is no more final because it is recent than it is true because it is modern. Those who
would put the dunce cap on Jesus, fool only themselves. The
humanist lives by commitments that are borrowed from theism
or he could not live as a human at all. While he may deny the
power of Christian realities in his own life, he cannot alter the
nature of the real world, nor can he banish enduring truth and a
fixed and final good. To the humanist, no less than to the rest of
us, Jesus offers a new identity in the eternal family of God's
people.

   I am not suggesting, of course, that Christians never do
anything foolish. While the New Testament declares Christ to
be the Wisdom of God, it speaks far more modestly of his disciples. We Christians can fall into human folly, and we do so
more often than we ought. "Do not be foolish," Paul exhorts the
Ephesian believers, "but understand what the Lord's will is"
(Ephesians 5:17). "Be very careful, then, how you live, not as
unwise but as wise" (5:15). Elsewhere he warns the Colossians:
"See to it that no one takes you captive through hollow and deceptive philosophy" (Colossians 2:8).

   Yet the folly of Christians should give no comfort to the
worldling. In his book *I Believe in the Creator*, onetime Oxford
professor James Houston puts the point well: "The Christian
goes about the world, tongue in cheek, as God's clown, knowing that the mask he wears on earth will one day become a real
face in heaven." Unwise though he may be at times, the Christian at least escapes condemnation as the fool of fools. He is not
the fool of whom Jesus spoke, the one who builds his future on

material rather than spiritual securities. The supreme fool is he to whom God says, "You fool! This very night your life will be demanded from you" (Luke 12:20).

We may seek to isolate Jesus from the mainstream of life, or, if we accommodate him at all, to do so only privately and not in public. But all who are embarrassed in his presence, and who may at times be tempted to whisper "he is beside himself," he boldly invites to join him in the new family of God. When he asks "Who is my mother? Who are my brothers?," he looks and waits for an answer, and leaves it to us to confess or deny him before men.

The Outrageous Evil of Abortion

*T*wo ironies surround the present controversy over abortion. First, in regard to physicians, it is remarkable that while surgeons such as Dr. C. Everett Koop have won fame in pediatric surgery by conquering congenital defects incompatible with life, and while biochemists are bending every effort to develop a living cell that can reproduce itself, the medical profession—although morally charged to preserve and protect life—now so readily lends itself to the willful destruction of normal fetuses by abortion. The situation among the clergy is no less astonishing. Today, many clergymen promote the elimination of all legal restriction of abortion, and in effect accommodate a revival of infanticide. Ancient Christianity, by contrast, clarified the distinction between right and wrong, revived the insensitive conscience of pagan parents who disposed of unwanted baby girls on public garbage heaps, and compassionately sought to lead the weak and unwanted to meaningful spiritual life in

Remarks at a seminar sponsored by the Christian Medical Society at its 21st annual Middle Atlantic States Regional Conference at Tenth Presbyterian Church, Philadelphia, 7 November 1970.

57

Christ. Are modern exponents of abortion-on-request less bar-
baric than their pagan Roman counterparts because their
methods of discarding infant life with the medical trash seem
more sophisticated?

I do not contend that no revision of abortion laws is necessary. Abortion laws are today woefully inconsistent, and revision is necessary. But I would emphasize that it is not the prime
role of the church, whether it approves or disapproves of abortion, to dictate the laws of the community. The church makes a
costly mistake whenever it compels the world to conform reluc-
tantly to what its own communion ought to do voluntarily; the
more so when its own communion is left unsure what Christian
morality requires. The clergy's task ought to be to illumine the
obscure line between morality and immorality. But precisely
this function is being neglected today by clergymen most vocal
in promoting abortion-on-request.

Many churchmen focus so intently on liberalization of
state laws that the public gets the misimpression that law created
the problem and is a worse evil than abortion itself. The
Methodist Board of Social Concerns called upon Methodist
agencies to "assist the states in removing the regulation of abortion from the criminal code" (Statement on Responsible Parent-
hood, October 8, 1969). The General Assembly of the United
Presbyterian Church in the U.S.A. not only accepted for a study
a report recommending the removal of abortion from all legal
answerability, but in a list of sexual sins such as adultery and
prostitution it refrained from mentioning abortion as sinful
under any circumstances whatever. I sometimes wonder what
counsel would have been given to Joseph and Mary by activist
churchmen informed of Mary's psychic visions, and their insistence that Joseph was not the father of Mary's expected babe. It
is not too radical to predict that a clergyman insensitive to biblical realities and holding modern permissive views of sex might
raise the subject of abortion and name a referral service.

If the fetus has developed to the point at which it can be
salvaged for human survival, despite premature birth, not to sal-
vage that life is an act of willful and wanton destruction. I am

told that such operations are now possible at the age of five months or a weight of about two pounds six ounces. Yet, Maryland permits abortion up to twenty-six weeks, and New York up to twenty-four weeks, while some proponents of abortion champion a woman's right to abort her baby at any stage of its prenatal development. The stage at which the life of the fetus can be prematurely removed is being steadily lessened; the invention of an artificial uterus might even make possible the preservation of the product of conception almost to the stage of fertilization.

If the life of a helpless fetus is forfeitable simply because parents sense no moral obligation to spare it and the mother wills its death, do the mother and father, in principle, forfeit any right to their own survival if they become helpless and their children are disposed to destroy them? If the decision to preserve or destroy rests upon personal convenience or social considerations such as overpopulation, is not the case even stronger for the child's disposal of a parent approaching senility?

Despite the effort to remove abortion from all public answerability, it is often argued that abortion serves the cause either of justice or of compassion. But if it serves the cause of justice, the public must understand how it bears on the question of personal and community rights. A woman's body is indeed not the property of others but is her own to control under God in responsible relation to society. But pregnancy indicates that she has shared her body and stands in relationship to a second and third party, and through these to society. Abortion cannot be catalogued with suicide as a merely personal decision, since the life involved is not the mother's own, and the question remains whether the fetus has its own right to life. If the attempt is made to justify abortion on grounds of compassion, compassion presupposes interpersonal relationships, and the question of the humanity or personality of the fetus cannot be ignored.

The arbitrary dictum that prenatal life is prehuman is objectionably simplistic. Life in the womb is not life as it exists after delivery, but it is human life in some form. This can be argued both biblically and medically. The psalmist writes:

Thou it was who didst fashion my inward parts;
thou didst knit me together in my mother's womb.

. . . .

Thou knowest me through and through:
    my body is no mystery to thee,
how I was secretly kneaded into shape
    and patterned in the depths of the earth.
Thou didst see my limbs unformed in the womb,
    and in thy book they are all recorded;
    day by day they were fashioned,
    not one of them was late in growing.
        (Psalm 139:13-16 NEB)

Medically, we know that the fetus receives its total genetic complement of RNA and DNA at conception, is a unique and unrepeatable combination of proteins, and is in some sense alive. By the end of four weeks—when the mother often first begins to suspect pregnancy—the heart has begun pumping. At eight weeks, all essential organ formations except the limbs are present, and the electrical activity of the fetal brain is already readable. The fetus responds to external stimuli long before it is capable of spontaneous motion at ten weeks. Professor Paul Ramsey of Princeton University pointedly asks why, if breath-of-life and brain activity are important considerations in deciding the exact moment for human death in removing organ transplants, they should not also be considered decisive for the beginnings of human life?

In view of the public implications of abortion, the community has a right to know and to exercise legal and moral judgment. If the citizenry has a right to know why on occasion a surgeon decides to save a pregnancy and to sacrifice the mother, the community has a right to also know why he sacrifices the pregnancy. But the church ought not to impose Christian morality upon the world in general; it ought rather by precept and example to exhibit the ethical principles of revealed religion. While the law does view abortion as legitimate when pregnancies are induced by rape or incest, when abortion is therapeutic, or when psychic deformity is radically extreme, for Christian ethics a decision regarding termination of a seriously defective fetus is not easy. But the argument that abortion is an ideal method of birth control is spurious; there are methods of birth control that avoid formation of the zygote. And the argument that the fetus becomes human only when the doctor spanks the baby's bottom at delivery is naive.

The clergy ought not to advocate, nor the medics to accommodate, the clamor for abortion-on-demand. Let the world advocate it and nonmedics as abortion-agents accommodate whatever is legal, if they choose; but let the clergy clarify the obscure line between right and wrong and the medics give themselves to the preservation and protection of life. Ours is a culture in which spiritually and morally sensitive leaders ought to be promoting the dignity of human life, rather than accommodating its destruction.

PART 2

THE PRESCRIPTION

The Greatest Text on Freedom

*M*y text is the greatest text on freedom: "You will know the truth, and the truth will set you free. . . . So if the Son sets you free, you will be free indeed" (John 8:32,36).

I have three points:

First, the world speaks of what is "free" and of "freedom," but there is always a catch or a snare.

Second, Christ speaks of what is "free indeed"; that is, of true freedom.

Third, the freedom promised by the world is not real freedom but bondage; only life in Christ is true freedom.

1. *The world says much about what is free and about freedom, but . . . beware!*

In the past year I have received letters telling me that I had won a two-week vacation in Hawaii, a stereo set, a new car, a new home near a beautiful lake, and $10,000 a year for life—all of them "free." That is, almost free; always there was some catch or trick. *If* I subscribe to a magazine, then *perhaps* I will be one of the lucky ones. *If* I visit a real estate resort, then

A sermon preached on Sunday, 4 July 1981, at the First Presbyterian Church of Berkeley, California.

perhaps I will win a new home or a new car. *If* this or that, then *maybe* I will be a lucky winner. Free . . . maybe!

Philosophers and politicians for many centuries have also promised a new world of freedom. In every generation people have been lured by the bait of hollow illusions.

The ancient Stoics promised freedom from fear of the external universe if only we change our inner attitude and outlook on things. That philosophy is still with us. Think positively! But freedom is not simply a matter of how we look at things. Freedom requires our right relation to God who works out his purposes in the external world, and who works in human history and in the lives of all who trust him. Freedom is not, in the last analysis, our own invention or creation.

The Communists take quite another tack. Trust their totalitarian rulers to define truth and justice and to stipulate freedoms and everything will be well, they say. They give the impression that the rest of us are enslaved while they are the vanguard of liberty. Sometimes they defame Christianity by saying that it took the Christians all of nineteen centuries to get rid of slavery. I recall a brilliant rejoinder by the distinguished missionary and church historian Sam Moffett. It may have taken Christians longer than it should have to get rid of slavery, said Moffett, but it took the Communists only one generation to bring it back. Read Solzhenitsyn's report of his prison experiences in the Russian gulag and you'll know what Moffett means.

But the Bible says: Let God be God! The living God does not authorize totalitarian rulers to redefine truth or the good, to redefine justice, or to redefine freedom. He himself stipulates right and wrong. He bestows upon human beings the freedom that is ideally theirs: "If the Son sets you free, you will be free indeed."

Secular humanists propose still another way. Surrender the supernatural and the myth of God, they say, and human beings will then be free to impose upon history and upon the cosmos the only values this world will ever bear. Man is his own lord in matters of truth and morality. The rejection of God, they say, is a necessary prelude to a right view of the dignity, worth, and freedom of man.

But to lose God (the Bible says) is to lose human worth and dignity, and to lose human freedom as well. It can never reinforce it! We are made in God's image; "the fool says in his heart, 'There is no God'" (Psalm 14:1). "You will know the truth," says the Bible, "and the truth will make you free." Evolutionary naturalism provides no basis either for the permanent or universal dignity of man. If everyone is his own lord, then man is free to enslave others, free to lie and cheat, free to love and leave, free to rape and run. Seek a godless freedom and we are all doomed.

Charles Malik, former chairman of the United Nations General Assembly, says that true freedom is the greatest promise that any nation can offer to the world, yet Western leaders, he says, now only rarely talk about it. Even in the so-called free world, people more and more treasure security or economic sufficiency or self-gratification more than they treasure freedom. Even among evangelical Christians in America, a recent *Christianity Today*–Gallup poll reveals that an astonishing number now consider personal security more important than freedom. Perhaps we value freedom so lightly because, unlike believers in Russia and China and Iran, we have not suffered for our faith.

Freedom is a noble and precious commodity. Beware of those who devalue freedom or connect it with vice and vanity, or try to snare you with beguiling conditions—free if you are lucky, free if you ignore God's will. They conjoin freedom only with your own strong desires, without accountability, without penalty for the abuse and misuse of it—freedom for drugs, freedom for fornication, freedom for exploitation of others. True freedom means liberty of the whole man, liberty of spirit, liberty of conscience; its antithesis is an enslaved spirit, slavery of the mind, slavery of the body, slavery of the whole man.

The world talks a great deal about what is free and about freedom, but there is always a hidden catch or a snare, a trap or a trick. The daughter of a country minister said to me recently after a church service, "I came to this city and for six months all my values have been pressured by young people who tell me to let go and run free. I needed what you said, because in my heart I knew that theirs is the way to bondage." Remember what Peter the apostle says about persons who promise us false freedom: "They mouth empty, boastful words and, by appealing to the lustful desires of sinful human nature, they entice people. . . . They promise them freedom, while they themselves are slaves of depravity—for a man is a slave to whatever has mastered him" (2 Peter 2:18ff). They offer you freedom, says Peter, but they can give you only bondage. Why? Because they themselves are in bondage. The world offers freedom . . . with a catch or a snare.

2. *Christ speaks of true freedom, of being free indeed*.

Free, period. Free, exclamation point! No tricks, no small print. Christ's freedom is simply and purely freedom, FREEDOM in capital letters.

There is no real freedom except the freedom that God offers and provides. The Greek text uses the word *ontos* ("indeed"). The word *ontos* does not appear often in the New Testament, but where it does appear it is important. So we read, for example, that "the people . . . all held that John [the Baptist] was a prophet *ontos*" (Mark 11:32)—that is, he was a prophet *in fact*. The Roman centurion who watches Jesus die on the cross comments: "This was a righteous man indeed" (Luke 23:47)—that is, he was *certainly* a righteous man. The angel at the tomb declares that "the Lord is risen indeed" (Luke 24:34)— that is, *it is true* that he arose. It's for real, no mistake about it. So when Christ declares, "If the Son will make you free, you will be free indeed," the text means *really free*, free *truly*, free *in reality*, free *in point of fact*, as opposed to what is pretended and fictitious.

Ring the bells! Stop the presses! Light the fireworks! Sound the bugles! Let a thousand trumpets blow! Put a rainbow in the sky! "If the Son will make you free, you will be *free indeed*"!

"Well, yes, but . . . " you say.

"Free *indeed*, says Jesus. It's the real thing, not a counterfeit—the freedom of the truly free. Iron chains fall away from mind and heart and will. Freedom in Christ is freedom without a bad conscience, freedom alive to a good conscience, freedom that thrives in knowledge that God is our friend and heaven is our destiny. Freedom is defined not by tyrants nor by your will nor mine, not by the will of the minority or even by the will of the majority. True freedom is defined by the will of God, by Christ who wants to make us *free indeed*. Christ offers us the real thing!

3. *The freedom promised by the world is not real freedom, but bondage; only life in Christ is real freedom.*

The service of God "is perfect freedom"—so reads the Anglican Book of Common Prayer. I am not saying that the cause of freedom as all humans conceive it is God's cause, but rather that God's cause is the cause of true freedom. Freedom is something heaven-made and heaven-given, something very real and definable, something we can know and experience. God created man free to do his holy will; Christ's redemption restores our now-broken freedom. Freedom in Christ means freedom from our rebellious will, it means a will reborn to God's will and ways. Abraham Lincoln spoke of "a new birth of freedom." That phrase has a biblical sense about it; freedom and new birth now profoundly imply each other. There is freedom in Christ; your Lord's name is freedom. To be sure, a struggle goes on even within the regenerate man or woman. But the apostle Paul insisted that "sin shall not be your master." Come to terms with Christ, for you will never be truly free until you make him Savior and King.

Freedom is whole and indivisible. Those who try to subdivide it and offer you only this crumb or that crumb of freedom sooner or later hurt themselves and us. Some speak only of "political freedom" or of "economic freedom" or of "scientific freedom," and each of these, properly understood, has immense importance. But real freedom is not something divisible; freedom subdivided is a compromise with bondage. Value anything else above the comprehensive freedom found in Christ and you will not only lose true freedom, but the fragmented freedoms you have will sooner or later give way because they are not self-supporting. Whittle away at freedom and gradually it will all be gone: freedom of belief, freedom of thought, freedom of expression, a free press, free elections, free enterprise, free movement and association, freedom from arbitrary arrest—all of it gone. Neglect the spiritual and moral foundations of freedom, and society itself will soon strip away the fragmented freedoms one by one. But if you have moral and spiritual freedom you can endure the loss of all else.

On a recent plane flight I happened into a friend from Hong Kong. He told me about a Chinese Christian who had gone to the mainland to visit his family and dreaded to learn of their fate under communist rule. He learned that all five—including an uncle who had been an atheist—had come to faith in Christ through house church ministries. Aflame with the unexpected moral and spiritual liberty they had found in Christ, they talked of this rather than of their political bondage.

Don't misunderstand me. Political liberty is important, very important. The right of political self-determination is a great treasure. It is all the more important in a world where totalitarian rulers hold many millions in political bondage and where dictators routinely repress the rights of people.

But its best friend is religious freedom, for religious freedom shelters all the other freedoms. Religious freedom gives you freedom not to worship Caesar, but to worship Caesar's God, the King of kings and Lord of lords. The living God guarantees all true freedoms—freedom to resist the caesars who would make themselves god, freedom from all myths about the tyranny of nature and history and about scientific determinism or cultural determinism or economic determinism. The isolated pursuit of political freedom soon defeats its own best intentions because it is too narrow a goal. Only where the people prize not merely their own will but the will of God above that of the ruler—and above that of the masses and above their own will also—will a nation endure. Political freedom has biblical roots. It does not last long unless the people help to preserve its spiritual and moral foundations; where those foundations are ignored, even the democracies fall into shame and scandal. In this very century that once hoped to achieve a universal extension of political freedom, that ideal is now being questioned by nations long obsessed by the hope of being liberated; even some so-called "free nations" now wonder how long freedom can survive.

The apostle Paul knew that Christ Jesus is King of kings, that Christ alone is the Lord of all right and of all human rights. To be sure, he appealed to Caesar to protect his rights as a Roman citizen; what he expected from Caesar was justice. Paul expected Caesar to promote justice because God is the source and stipulator of right and of justice. Human rights and duties are grounded in God's creation of man and in God's ordination of civil government to preserve the justice that God prescribes, not to promote the self-interest of the rulers or of the governed.

What a travesty on justice that in a world empire noted for law and order, Jesus of Nazareth was crucified under a procurator who had declared him innocent, and that in that same empire the apostle Paul at the height of his career was taken out of the Mamertine prison and beheaded by a ruler and a people who held that Caesar was God.

Remove the living God from the life of a nation and all its secondary liberties soon become an illusion. Even in the present controversy over capitalism, socialism, and communism, that principle holds true. The modern debate over ultimates is being waged on too narrow a strip. We must challenge Marxist reduction of all issues to material-economic-physical categories. We cannot really win out unless we deal with the supremacy of spiritual values and with the nature of morality and justice—with the purposes for which God wills our freedom—and with the proper relationship of man and government. The sad truth, Charles Malik says (and he is right), is that "the whole climate of opinion today" is materialistic and relativistic. In his address at Harvard University a few years ago, Aleksandr Solzhenitsyn scored the same point: the very freedom that the West offers to the Soviet world has already accommodated the materialism, the decadence, and the criminality that spells the loss of human worth and invites the end of modern civilization.

Jesus said, "you will know the truth and the truth will make you free." The Word of God does not turn magnificent biblical terms—like truth, freedom, hope, justice, and love—into cheap propaganda slogans. The big barrier to freedom, the apostle Peter says, is man's enslavement to depravity, that is, the sinfulness of human nature. Those who are "slaves to corruption" (JB) cannot give us freedom. No matter what aspect of freedom we consider, a will bent against God's will invites bondage. All this world's many claims about freedom, the Bible says, come to "great swelling words of vanity" (KJV)—or as the modern translations put it—they are "high-flown talk" (JB), "loud boasts of folly" (RSV), "big, empty words" (NEB), "proud and stupid statements" (TEV). Freedom that ignores moral and spiritual bondage soon collapses into rubble.

The Bible deals with sin at the core of human life. It offers us freedom through Christ. Christ frees us from sin's power and guilt and penalty. He frees us from spiritual death. He frees us from separation from God. He frees us by his substitutionary death and resurrection life. He offers freedom from self, from a mind and will and heart set against the will of God. He offers us freedom from the law's power to condemn us in our sins. Christ frees us from all ghastly terrors and offers freedom for God and the good. He offers freedom to will and to do the good as never before. He offers freedom for truth—freedom to think God's thoughts after him. He offers freedom for love—that reaches to the needs of others as to a brother or to a sister. He offers freedom for justice—to stand with the helpless outcast in the name of the justice God demands. Christ offers freedom for hope—freedom for the coming resurrection of the righteous and for heaven as our home. He offers us *freedom*.

Century after century and generation after generation, the Bible has been the great Book of Freedom with a mighty, liberating message. The epistle to the Romans alone, in which

Paul speaks of justification by faith and of government under God, has registered an incomparable influence for freedom upon influential leaders of thought and life. When Augustine heard the voice *Tolle, lege!* ("Take and read!"), the book of Romans became the inspiration for his great work on *The City of God and the City of Man*. Paul's letter to the Romans also loosed Martin Luther from his tortuous struggle for salvation by works and sparked the Protestant Reformation. Early in our century Karl Barth's reading of Romans freed him from the misconceptions of theological modernism, which he then deplored as heresy while he called instead—even if in a confusing way—for a new hearing of the transcendent Word of God.

In the history of letters, there is probably no more astounding coupling of words than those at the very beginning of Romans. First stands Paul's name, in keeping with the custom of that day when writers identified themselves not at the end of correspondence, but at the outset. Even Paul's own name, in Latin, means "little"; and that of itself would hardly impress imperious Romans. But what term does Paul then add to his own name? Neither Plato nor Aristotle nor any other world philosopher of ancient times or of modern times would have used it alongside his own name. If one wanted friends among Roman nobles and scholars, wanted to win personal favor and influence, who would ever have used that word? Here is what Paul writes: *Paulos doulos*, that is, Paul a slave, a servant, a servant of Jesus Christ (Romans 1:1). As the Living Bible puts it, "Paul, Jesus Christ's slave."

Paul had found a freedom unknown to the law-ridden Jew and unknown to the philosophy-fascinated Gentile, a freedom unknown to Greeks and Romans and lost by most of the Hebrews: freedom that God gives. This freedom he found in the crucified and risen Jesus, freedom that comes through the life and death and activity of Jesus Christ, through Messiah's work of atonement for our sins and the liberating, life-giving power of the Holy Spirit. This freedom allows us to be what the Creator intends us to be, namely, the children of God in a new society of mankind.

How is it with you? Remain in moral and spiritual bondage and you lose everything, even those beggarly freedoms that cannot sustain themselves. Until Christ rules your life, you will never be personally free. God defines the good, the true, the right, the just, and he calls men and nations to do his will. He invites you to come to terms with Christ, with the Lord of the nations and of history and of all mankind. Christ will judge the nations—America, Russia, England, and every other; he will judge us all personally. Be free, says Jesus—free for God and the good and the right! Off with the chains! "If the Son sets you free, you will be free indeed." *Paulos doulos*, Jesus Christ's servant—so writes the great apostle. "A man is a slave to whatever has mastered him," says the Bible. Be free, says Jesus: know the truth, for the truth shall make you free. "If the Son sets you free, you will be free *indeed*." Free from the penalty and guilt and power of sin. Free for God and the good. Free. Free! *Free!*

True Liberation

*L*iberation is the modern motif: Chinese leaders speak of cultural liberation, Latin Americans have a liberation theology, Americans talk much today about women's liberation.

Our text depicts a multiliberated woman—liberated from race prejudice, from religious prejudice, from sexual prejudice, and from social prejudice. The liberating power of a personal relationship to Jesus Christ is incomparable. I have seen nothing as awesome and rewarding in a million or more miles of air travel around the earth as the liberation Jesus Christ brings into human experience.

Jesus canceled the ongoing inner emptiness that drained the Samaritan woman's life of personal meaning and worth. He offered her new possibilities in place of problems that she little suspected lay at the bottom of her life. The special path of sin she traveled was sexual license, which now has become a way of life for many moderns. But she was a modern woman before our times in a deeper and unsuspected way—she lacked a

---

An exposition of John 14:1-42 presented to teaching leaders of the Bible Study Fellowship in San Antonio on 18 June 1985.

spiritual vision of life. Her materialistic life-orientation robbed her of power to serve the living God and to be true to a higher selfhood. She held a naturalistic, empirical, sensate outlook, interested in this-worldly things and events, and not in the things of the Spirit.

The whole drama took place in Sychar, a small country town. America's little villages have been the butt of enough jokes to well imagine that Sychar was not exempt from caricature. During part of my boyhood I lived in a small country town, yet one big enough so that when the train stopped, the engineer didn't have to choose between thrusting his engine into the next village or trailing his caboose in the last. In ancient Sychar the problem may rather have been which end of the donkey to park in suburbia.

Yet almost every hamlet offers something distinctive, even if only a rationalization of why townspeople wouldn't move elsewhere should the opportunity arise. As for Sychar, it had a tourist attraction for strangers: Jacob's well, near the parcel of ground for which it was named (which Jacob had given to his son Joseph, vv. 5-6). I suspect that some of you have seen it, for it is still there. The well supplied water that was considered choice; if public relations men had been in business on the Samaritan Road, they probably would have promoted it as a "supernatural thirst-quencher." At least the Sycharians, including this woman, emphasized that Jacob "gave us the well and drank from it himself, as did also his sons, and his flocks and herds" (v. 12). It was not a cistern storing stagnant water, but was fed by hidden springs whose refreshing waters bubbled with Old Testament memories reaching back to the patriarchs. What better place to turn than Jacob's well when life was parched by drought?

Sychar did not escape the prejudices of the outside world, and the Sycharians themselves had local prejudices based on scandal and gossip. Some of these prejudices were but surface scars, others were deep and festering.

The Jewish religious leaders disdained not only the

Samaritan religion, but also the Samaritan people because of their break with the prophetic tradition: "For Jews do not associate with Samaritans" (v. 9). Consequently, Jews going to Galilee would take the long route east of Jordan to avoid contact with the Samaritans. But Jesus, you recall, was constrained to go through Samaria (v. 4). The road he charts to Galilee foregleams the Great Commission; all nations, all mankind, are on his agenda. The problem of Jesus' disciples was not anti-Semitism but anti-Samaritanism. While the disciples could adjust to some minimal dealings with the Samaritans (if absolutely necessary), the fewer such encounters the better. We read that they had already gone into the city "to buy food" (v. 8), maybe to a kosher butcher, though probably just for ordinary foodstuffs. The Samaritan woman, meanwhile, easily spotted Jesus as a Jew, for he had the visible outward marks of Jewishness. (Remember Jesus the next time you see a Jew.) Because Jews disdained the Samaritans, the Samaritan woman was perplexed by Jesus' approach to her ("Will you give me a drink?").

Some modern commentators see sex in everything, and they think the Samaritan woman—who was not lacking in sexuality—was a cheap prostitute who at first may have thought Jesus was propositioning her. Yet nothing in the exchange of conversation and its implications indicates that she was as sex-oriented as are some of today's interpreters, who seem unable to get sex off their minds. Discrimination against women has many important things to be said against it, although those who make the most noise are not always its victims. The modern male tendency to see a pair of limbs, or a bosom, or a sex object rather than a human person might well recall Jesus' eloquent warning in the Sermon on the Mount: "Anyone who looks at a woman lustfully has already committed adultery with her in his heart" (Matthew 5:28). It ought also to put women on guard against escalating sexually-oriented expectations.

At Jacob's well, there is nonetheless a sex-oriented surprise at the very outset. Jesus' words were doubly remarkable because he addressed not only a Samaritan, but a woman: "You are a Jew and I am a Samaritan woman. How can you ask me for a drink?" (v. 9). The role of women in the ancient world was incredibly servile. Even Jesus' disciples at their return from Sychar "were surprised to find him talking with a woman" (v. 27).

The reason Jesus spoke to her seemed prompted by a very basic human need—thirst. Weary with the journey, he stopped at high noon and sat at the well. Since the well was a hundred feet deep and he had nothing to draw with (v. 11), he waited there for a water carrier. When the Samaritan woman approached, he entreated her for water: "Will you give me a drink?" (v. 7). She was amazed that a Jew would ask her, a Samaritan (and a woman at that!), for water, and that he would have any dealings whatever with her, even the sharing of a common vessel. That amazement became for Jesus an open door to declare God's amazing grace.

Not only does he ask of her, but he jolts her even more with the suggestion that she should ask of him for living water, which incredibly, he would give her: "If you knew the gift of God and who it is that asks you for a drink, you would have asked him and he would have given you living water" (v. 10)— that is, running water, gushing water. He may even imply culpability because she had not taken an initiative: "I would have given . . . if you only knew and asked." He excites her curiosity concerning the gift and the giver. The gift is the Spirit of God, and "who it is" is the Son by whom the Spirit is bestowed; that is one of the great New Testament doctrines. The outpoured Spirit of God is the gift, and Jesus himself is the divine bucket! The Spirit gives eternal life and quenches our thirst for things that cannot permanently satisfy.

The Samaritan woman's reply discloses her real predicament—she suffers not simply from colossal spiritual blindness, but from a materialistic and naturalistic misunderstanding of life. It is inherently impossible for Jesus to give her anything more potent than the traditions she already has. "Sir," the woman said, "you have nothing to draw with and the well is deep." Hence, the utter impossibility is two-fold: the existing circumstances and Jesus' own lack of reach—it seemed totally incredible that Jesus could give her better water.

The Samaritan woman is not too far removed in outlook from the secular modern man or woman who transmutes all spiritual truth into material and naturalistic concerns. She thinks of water only in terms of H_2O, and the lack of adequate technology is the only barrier to supplying it. Profess to pity her though we may, we moderns are often leagued in spirit with this Samaritan woman; indeed, she anticipates the very mood of modernity.

There remains one remote alternative, a possibility too unthinkable to mention except by way of rhetorical question: "Are you greater . . . ?" Indeed, the phrasing virtually expects a negative answer: "You aren't greater, are you . . ." (than Marx? . . . than Darwin? . . . than Freud? . . . than dialectical materialism . . . or psychoanalysis . . . or whatever else—all the more tragic in her case that the prophetic Old Testament gets in the way)—"than our father Jacob, who gave us the well and drank from it himself, as did also his sons, and his flocks and herds?"

"You aren't greater, are you . . . ?" Greater than what? Greater than what we already have, greater than our own resources? Our problems—long-standing ones, that drive men and women to the well every day, to barbiturates, to drink, to drugs, to any cult that promises relief—are you greater than these? The hidden problems that hurt too much to look them in the face, the repressed anxieties, the burdens people store up for a psychiatrist to surface—the well is deep—you aren't greater, are you?

What Jesus says is twice as powerful in the Greek than in the standard English versions. "Everyone who drinks this water will be thirsty again, but whoever drinks the water I give him will never thirst" (v. 14a). Jesus says: "Whoever drinks (once: aorist) the water I give will never (never at all: double negative) thirst." Then he adds: "Indeed, the water I give him will become in him a spring of water (literally, an artesian well) welling up to eternal life" (v. 14).

The Samaritan woman leaped to the offer in a profound misunderstanding. She screens the entire conversation through sensate, materialistic, physical categories: no more daily trips to the well, no more arduous carrying of the waterpots, but rather a built-in reservoir that will never run low. "Sir, give me this water so that I won't get thirsty and have to keep coming here to draw water" (v. 15). Her heart throbs to the relief of this-worldly cares with no concern whatever for the invisible spiritual world; she sifts out every intimation of the eternal and ethical.

That is why Jesus now triggers head-on the moral problem in her life, in as abrupt a turn of conversation as can be found anywhere in his discourses: "Go, call your husband and come back" (v. 16). There is a moral block in her life, and only the Holy Spirit can flush it out and flood her heart with righteousness and hope and joy. Jesus calls her to face up with reality—the inescapable reality of God, the inescapable reality of truth, the inescapable reality of judgment. The water of life cannot flow through a polluted channel without cleaning it up. The only way to say "Give me this water" with integrity is to come clean with the confession, "I have no husband" (v. 17)—to come clean with it, and not simply in a conversational saunter or shield from shame.

Jesus' reply leaves no doubt that there was a moral scandal. Clearly she had something to hide. Even the rabbis in Jesus' day, with all their ingenuity in interpreting the law, considered three marriages the limit under any circumstances. This woman had been married five times and now had some other arrangement. Five husbands and another man to boot takes quite a bit of coverup and camouflage, particularly if by saying, "I have no husband," she means to hide her private life from Jesus.

Yet, I am not going to prejudge her. It's easy enough for a man to blame the woman. There isn't a word in this text that puts the blame fully on her doorstep. Had the men in her life deceived her? To what desperate measures of survival was she perhaps driven when nobody else would help? To blame or not, she recognizes that divine knowledge had exposed the moral dilemma that had become her life, and she acknowledges: "Sir, I can see that you are a prophet" (v. 19).

What she does next suggests that she is morally embarrassed and has a bad conscience. She turns the presence of the prophet into an occasion for pursuing a theological problem. When people are pressed to the wall with the need for moral renewal and spiritual decision, for forgiveness of sins and new life, they often will trot out all the theological dilemmas they can muster—the Virgin Birth, the Resurrection, the Flood, you name it—before making a clean breast of things. The Samaritan woman turns away from conscience to a debate about the history of religion: "Our fathers worshiped on this mountain, but you Jews claim that the place where we must worship is in Jerusalem" (v.20). That long-standing historical debate reached back to Deuteronomy (12:5, 11ff.). The Samaritans rejected the prophetic writings, and restricted themselves to the Pentateuch.

Now, while a theological question can be difficult, the answer need not be oblique; it is possible to hold together truth and righteousness and grace in a way that pushes compromise to the wall. The place to worship is, for many people today, still a basic religious problem, and some opt for no place at all. But Jesus emphasizes three great themes: (1) True religion centers in the proper object of worship, the living God of prophetic promise: "You Samaritans worship what you do not know, we worship what we do know, for salvation is from the Jews" (v. 22). (2) True worship is spiritual, not geographical: "God is spirit, and his worshipers must worship in spirit and in truth" (v. 24). (3) True religion has promise and fulfillment at its heart: "A time is coming when you will worship the Father neither on this mountain nor in Jerusalem." (v. 21). Even the Jerusalem temple, forty-six years in building, was to give way to the temple raised up in three days. Thereafter humans would worship God wherever they are, through Jesus Christ the Mediator. "Yet a time is coming and has now come," Jesus says—his voice trembling on the brink of the hour when he could cry "It is finished!"—"when the true worshipers will worship the Father in spirit and truth, for they are the kind of worshipers the Father seeks" (v. 23). God wants us not simply to come to a place, but to come to him personally for the redemption, for the living water, that he offers.

The Samaritan woman replies that she is aware that the coming Messiah is to inaugurate the new era of worship: "I know," she says, "that Messiah" (called Christ) "is coming. When he comes, he will explain everything to us" (v. 25).

"I who speak," says Jesus, in a dramatic moment of Messianic self-disclosure, "I who speak to you am he" (v. 26). Here is the first of the great I AM declarations of the fourth gospel. "I AM . . . he," that is, the Messiah. "I am the bread that came down from heaven"; "I am the light of the world"; "I am the resurrection and the life." All this and more is anticipated in the words, "I am the Messiah . . . I am the giver of living water"! In John 7:37f. we read that on the last day of the feast "Jesus stood and said in a loud voice, 'If any one is thirsty, let him come to me and drink. Whoever believes in me, as the Scripture has said, streams of living water will flow from within him.' By this he meant the Spirit . . . ."

At this very moment of Jesus' disclosure—"if you knew the gift of God and who it is . . . you would have . . ." (v. 10), the disciples return and marvel that Jesus is talking with the Samaritan woman (v. 27). Meanwhile the woman leaves and returns to the city (v. 28). Rabbinic writings carry the statement, "Burn the Law rather than talk to a woman in public!" We have no way of telling whether the woman sensed what Jesus' disciples thought; the text says they "were surprised . . . But no one asked, 'What do you want? or 'Why are you talking with her?'" (v. 27). They played it cool both ways—no implied criticism of Jesus, no show of compassion for the woman.

Some things, however, attest what had transpired in the very soul of the Samaritan woman: "[She] went back to the town and said to the people, 'Come, see a man . . .'" (v. 28f.). She knew the men of the city well; now she had met a man unlike any man she had ever met, a man she knew no man could afford to ignore, any more than she herself could: "Come, see a man . . . ." He "told me every thing I ever did. Could this be the Christ?" (v. 29).

Where else can all the past be unveiled with high hope except in the context of amazing grace? Jesus' word about her past arraigned her in the court of divine judgment, yet his word about the gift of God was a clear invitation to forgiveness of sins and to new life.

She now led the men of Sychar to the Messiah, for we read "they came out of the town, and made their way toward him" (v. 30). The Samaritan woman had stirred a sociological crisis—a crisis in the community—for she made Jesus Christ an issue in public conscience and life where people had watched her rot morally and spiritually, and some had contributed to her decline.

During our year in Cambridge, England, we came to know an English couple whose modest suburban home in Foxton was like a flowing well of witness, open night after night to people of the community. One night their home was open for Bible study, the next night for prayer, another night for a hymn sing, another for testimony, another for dialogue with humanists and atheists. Michael and Pauline Young were saying to their community: "Come, see a man . . . !" Among those converted at their home was a woman who had been for thirty years a member of the local Methodist Church. Her conversion made Christ an issue in all the area churches, for people thought it was impossible that someone would need conversion who had been a member of a church for that many years. People everywhere contrive their own impossibilities. The one raised by the woman at the well is still among them: "Are you greater . . . ?" (v. 12). Jesus' answer is still valid and clear, "If you knew . . . ." (v. 10).

The disciples, you remember, had been busy with necessary material concerns—provender for the day—and urged Jesus to take nourishment saying, "Rabbi, eat something" (v. 31). But he answered, "I have food to eat that you know nothing about" (v. 32). Perhaps his colleagues inferred that someone else had supplied Jesus with lunch (v. 33). Jesus makes the matter perfectly clear: "My food is to do the will of him who sent me, and to finish his work" (v. 34).

Nothing fills the heart and life with greater joy than leading someone to the living God and to new life in Christ. It was not only Jesus who had "food to eat" of which the disciples were unaware; the Samaritan woman had water to drink—living water—of which she had been unaware and which now satisfied her as none before it. In a dramatic touch of artistry, the gospel tells us that she left "her water jar . . . and went back to the town" (v. 28). Having carried her burden mile upon mile, she now had found water to drink that she knew not of.

Evangelistic opportunity is dramatically portrayed by Jesus when he connects a small planting of the gospel with the reaping of a considerable harvest. In the kingdom of God, he says to the disciples—who had just been into that city and brought back material provender but no converts, and who had wondered why Jesus was talking with the woman at the well—it is different than in the kingdom of nature. In nature one must wait four months after seedtime to harvest a crop. "I tell you," he says, as he sees the woman returning down the hill from Sychar accompanied by a group of her townspeople, their white garments glistening in the afternoon sun, "open your eyes and look at the fields! They are ripe for harvest" (v. 35). In the kingdom of God there can be mass harvests from individual plantings.

Now the disciples also had an opportunity to become spiritual harvesters. "Even now the reaper draws his wages, even now he harvests the crop for eternal life, so that the sower and the reaper may be glad together. Thus the saying 'One sows and another reaps' is true. I sent you to reap what you have not worked for. Others have done the hard work, and you have reaped the benefits of their labor" (vv. 36-38). Could it perhaps be that, alongside the woman's forsaken waterpot, the disciples also placed their own half-eaten bread and shared with Jesus that "food to eat" which they had not suspected, the inner refreshment of leading the lost to salvation?

At any rate, some things that happened are clear. In Sychar, a group of Samaritans had become believers in a single day: "Many of the Samaritans from that town believed in him" (v. 39). But that is not all! They were won to faith not by a miracle, but by the testimony of a Samaritan woman—the least likely carrier of the message of salvation in all the city. They believed, we read, "because of the woman's testimony, 'He told me everything I ever did'" (v. 39). The disciples had entered Sychar with cash for foodstuffs, and they left it spiritually as empty as when they had come. Moreover, when they peered at the Samaritan woman at the well, they regarded her as out of Jesus' league and theirs. But now the people of Sychar offered the key to the city not to them but to Jesus: "So when the Samaritans came to him they urged him to stay with them, and he stayed two days" (v. 40).

As a result, after hearing Jesus, "many more became believers" (v. 41), and declared, "we have heard for ourselves, and we know that this man really is the Savior of the world" (v. 42).

America is our Sychar. Let us "look at the fields . . . " of cities and hamlets with their social problems, sexual exploitation, race prejudice, religious differences, and much more. "Come, see a man" armed with a well springing up into everlasting life! Find food to eat better than any of this earth's best gourmet restaurants.

"Come, see a man . . ."!

Christ at the Center

*F*ew experiences intimidate me more than driving for the first
time over one of the world's great bridges. I still remember
my first encounter with George Washington Bridge in New
York City, Golden Gate Bridge in San Francisco, and the Firth
Bridge in windswept Scotland.

There is, however, an even more awesome bridge to ma-
neuver than the engineering feats of modern technology. It is a
bridge found in Paul's great letter to the Colossians, a bridge
that connects the first chapter with the rest of the epistle. More
expressly, it links a compact introduction about the supremacy
of Jesus Christ—his person and work—with a much longer
statement of the consequences of his life and mission for you
and for me.

The bridge is composed of three simple words. In my long
ministry, only once have I heard anybody preach on it. More
than thirty-five years ago, Dr. Wilbur M. Smith, whom I rank
with the most gifted Bible expositors of our century, did so one
night in a small suburban Midwest church. We shared the

Fall convocation message given at Westminster Seminary of California, in
Escondido, California, 7 September 1984.

platform for the installation of a new pastor. Dr. Smith gave the charge to the pastor, and I gave the charge to the church. I remember almost nothing of what I said. But Wilbur Smith's message so exalted Christ that I have long wanted to expound this text.

The three-word bridge, found in Colossians 1:28, is the transitional phrase *whom we preach*, to quote the venerable King James Version. It thrusts upon us, as I see it, three great concerns: (1) the centrality of Christ; (2) the priority of preaching; (3) and the maintenance of a mission.

First, who holds center stage? Who is in the spotlight? Jesus Christ is, and none other, "*whom* we preach." "*Him* we proclaim," says the Revised Standard Version; "*He it is* whom we proclaim," says the Jerusalem Bible. Take your pick of versions, the matter is clear: Jesus Christ stands at the summit; he is the sum and substance of our message.

Not somebody or something *other than Jesus*. Not a system of speculative philosophy to which we append Jesus as a footnote. Not some secret wisdom reserved for a few initiates and unavailable to the masses. Not some grand scheme of ethics. Not a religious ritual or discipline or yoga that claims to bring man near to God. Not even Christianity, but Christ; unless Christ is at the center, Christianity is a lost cause.

What shall we say then of Jesus Christ? He is supreme and unique in the whole world of being. His person and work attest it. He is intrinsically divine; he eternally preexists the space-time universe; he is the divine agent in the creation of the heavens and the earth; he supplies the cohesion and meaning and purpose of the universe; and *in him* God manifests all the splendor of divinity.

Hear the word of Scripture concerning the supremacy of Christ's person:

He is "*the image of the invisible God*" (v. 15). Jesus Christ is God's true and enduring image. Man was *made* in some respects to bear God's image by creation, though he is now fallen and flawed, and the image is warped. But Jesus Christ is not *made* in the image of God; he *is* the divine image.

Morever, he is *"the firstborn over all creation"* (v. 15); he has primacy over the universe. Whatever this phrase may mean—and even profound Greek scholars disagree—it puts immense distance between Jesus Christ and the entire created universe. It seems to indicate that Christ stands in a relationship of priority over creation, that he has the primacy that belongs to the firstborn, and this accords well with the next two statements.

"For by him all things were created: things in heaven and on earth, visible and invisible, whether thrones or power or rulers or authorities; all things were created *by him* and *for him."* (v. 16). Not only the visible universe but the invisible realm of heavenly beings as well—the angelic hosts included—were created *by him* as the agent in creation, and *for him* as the goal for which all creation exists.

"He is before all things, and *in him* all things hold together" (v. 17). He is not only prior to all the created universe, not only the divine agent in its creation, but the divine agent also in the preservation of the universe. Phillips paraphrases: "He is both the first principle and the upholding principle of the whole scheme of creation." He is the unifying principle, the personal sustainer of it all. The universe is held together not merely by gravity, by impersonal causation, but by personal sovereign will.

He is, moreover, the one in whom "God was pleased to have all his fullness dwell" (v. 19). He is endowed by the Holy Spirit not merely more than others are; the fullness of divinity is in him, and that not simply sporadically but continually, for he is the dwelling-place of the divine essence. False teachers at Colossae spoke of transcendent intermediary powers whose fullness controls human fortunes. But Paul affirms that in Jesus Christ dwells all that it means to be God. The modern German philosopher Hegel speculated that his Absolute did not pour fullness into any single form. But Paul declares that God the Father willed that all fullness should reside in Christ; in Jesus the very fullness of God resides.

In a day when God is caricatured by the crude images of our callous culture, Christ perfectly preserves and perpetuates the divine image. In a day when impersonal processes—quarks and quasars—are given the primacy, Jesus Christ stands as the first-born of all creation and the sovereign creator of all things and powers. In a day when humanism considers history and nature haphazard, purposeless, and directionless, Christ remains the upholding and unifying principle of the universe which exists through him and for him. In a day when the world is crammed with evil, the fullness of the Godhead dwells in Jesus Christ who stands in incomparable relationships both to the Godhead and to the universe. The divine essence is his; he precedes the universe in time and surpasses it in rank; he is the agent in its creation and the sustainer of it; he supplies its unity and meaning, and is its final goal.

But that is not all! Alongside the supremacy of Christ's person stands the supremacy of his work. His redemptive work bears not only upon the church, but upon the whole creation, anticipating the coming new creation. But before moving from Christ's person to his work, note with me that twice in this majestic chapter Paul stresses the electing purpose of the Godhead. All that he depicts about Jesus Christ is grounded in God's eternal plan. In verse 19 he says *God was pleased* that all fullness should dwell in Jesus Christ, and also that it *pleased the Father* to reconcile all things to himself by Jesus Christ.

Hear then the word of Scripture concerning the supremacy of his work:

"He is the head of the body, the church" (v. 18a). He exists in vital union with the church. More than that, he is its living head. Jesus Christ is head; not the Holy See, or an ecclesiastical magistracy, or a world ecumenical central committee.

He is head, moreover, because "he is the beginning and the firstborn from among the dead" (v. 18b). The Crucified One conquered death and, risen and exalted, he is the source of the church's life and power. Earlier, Paul had referred to Christ as *firstborn* "over all creation"—as prior in sovereignty and time. Now he emphasizes that Christ was first to conquer death in resurrection life, and this victory establishes his preeminence over the coming new creation as well as over the passing present one.

He has carried human nature into the eternal order, and from there he even now mediates to the church powers and virtues that anticipate the age to come.

When Paul concludes verse 18 with the crescendo, "So that *in everything* he might have the supremacy," we should note two things. First, the emphatic "he" *(autos)*. The Greek pronoun is usually implicit in the verb, but by its explicit use here, Paul underscores that it is Christ, Christ *himself*, Christ *alone*, who holds first place. Second, while this supremacy is linked with his resurrection, it also flows from all that is said about Christ's person and work.

In verse 14, Paul had already spoken of Jesus' work in that powerfully succinct statement about Christ's liberation of sinners: "*in whom* we have redemption, the forgiveness of sins." Great is the cost of our emancipation from sin's penalty and power: Christ himself redeemed us. Christ is not merely the agent in redemption; he is himself the Redeemer. (The phrase "through his blood" at this point in the King James Version has poor textual support; probably a scribe inserted it here as an echo of Ephesians 1:7 where there is firm textual support.) Yet by Christ's own death, by the shedding of his blood, we are indeed emancipated. In verses 19-23 Paul speaks further of the reconciling work of Christ, and at that point he expressly refers to "the blood of the cross": "For God was pleased to have all his fullness dwell in him, and *through him* to reconcile to himself all things, whether things on earth or things in heaven, by making peace through his blood, shed on the cross" (vv. 19-20).

The Father, who willed that all fullness dwell *in Christ*, willed likewise to "reconcile to himself all things" *in Christ*. The significance of Christ's work touches "all things"—everything in this universe. The created order will finally be wholly subdued to Christ's will and subordinated to his purpose. Yet Paul does not say that all humanity will be saved; in fact, he teaches the opposite. But Christ's work nonetheless has cosmic implications; his atonement will restore divine harmony to the universe. Our redemption is part of a mighty moral purpose that Christ is implementing. The reconciliation achieved by the

incarnate Son of God reverses man's spiritual rebellion and en-
trenches us in the household of God.

"He has reconciled you by Christ's physical body through
death to present you *holy* in his sight, without blemish and free
from accusation . . ." (vv. 22). Christ is interested in our holi-
ness, in our perfection and maturity. Believers will be presented
perfect because of what Christ has done, because of the person
and work of Christ. But the largest part of the Colossian letter
expounds what it means for a Christian to live as a Christian in
the society in which God has placed him. To live as Christians
is to live as "Christ's ones" in the world.

In summary, Christ is the *who* or *whom* at the center of it
all. The pronouns from verses 13 to 23 overwhelm us with the
supremacy of Christ: "he has," "in whom we have," "he is," "by
him," "by him and for him," "in him," "so . . . he might have,"
"through him," "to himself," "in his sight." *He, him, whom*:
everywhere Christ is indispensable; without him the bridge collapses. "We proclaim *him*."

Second, this same Christ, writes Paul, is the theme of
evangelical *preaching*: "we *proclaim* him." Christ, who is central in God's cosmic purpose and in God's redemptive purpose,
is to be central also in proclamation. The centrality of Christ
leads on to his priority in preaching. The world must be told that
Christ holds primal significance in the universe and in the
church and in respect to the destiny of all human beings.

Notice in verse 28 the three-fold "every man" (RSV). The
message is not the exclusive privilege of some secret cult, something to be monopolized by a spiritual elite. The truths of Chris-
tology are not to be confined to theology textbooks or to seminary classrooms or even to Christian studies programs, as if they
were merely of antiquarian or historical interest. The truth about
Christ must be proclaimed to the whole world.

"Him we *proclaim,* warning every man and teaching
every man in all wisdom, that we may present every man mature
in Christ" (RSV). The Greek word translated "preach" or "proclaim" is *katagellomen*. It may have a significance somewhat
wider than the more usual word for preach, *kerussō*. In any

case, we are dealing with the vocabulary of mission. There is a network-bulletin urgency: a crucially important event has transpired and people need to know. Having been a news reporter and editor, I know what that involves.

A mystery hidden for ages and generations is now dispelled, its glorious riches made known to Gentiles as well as to Jews. The Word of God is therefore to be made known in all its fullness. Not only does the gospel embrace the Gentiles also in its offer of redemption, but Christ himself personally indwells believers: "Christ in you, the hope of glory" (v. 27). The promised Messiah has come; the Crucified One is risen; the Lord who controls the sluicegates of eternity is the source of the believer's life, and personally indwells the people of God.

Christ is to be proclaimed and published, to be heralded publicly as crucially important news. Small wonder that Martyn Lloyd-Jones, that pulpit giant of Westminster Chapel, London, commented in his book *Preaching and Preachers* that "the work of preaching is the highest and the greatest and the most glorious calling to which anyone can ever be called."

The text connects preaching Christ with two important aspects—warning the nonbeliever and teaching the believers. This preaching has direction and depth, and no human being is exempt from its message. Its goal is to "present everyone perfect in Christ Jesus." It counsels against error and carefully articulates the truth so that the believer, united to Christ, will be spiritually mature or complete at Christ's return.

Preaching that has Christ as its center will keep us from lifting ourselves to centrality. We are not to preach personal experience, with Christ on the periphery. Rather, we must preach Jesus Christ, who makes evangelical experience possible. People in the pews may thirst for some morsel of evangelical gossip or for some biographical tidbit; they may even expect a bit of name-dropping, or want to hear the worst about some backsliding evangelical effort. But we are to give centrality to the Name that is above every other name. "We do not preach ourselves, but Jesus Christ," Paul writes to the Corinthians (2 Corinthians 4:5).

The greatest disaster for the evangelical cause is not when sound institutions begin to drift doctrinally, shameful as that is. Is it not far worse when efforts that profess and intend to be loyal blur their focus on Christ? The future of evangelical religion depends upon clarity over the identity and nature of the Savior of the world. Methods and means and mechanics have their place. But if the Mediator is not central to our preaching, we have lost touch with apostolic Christianity and with Christ. There can be only one reason for the perpetually discouraged condition of some churches: Christ is not at the center of the preaching. The priority of preaching and the centrality of Christ are two of the three main girders comprising the magnificent bridge found in our text. The great need of the church and of the world today is powerful preaching that has a missionary tone, that exalts Christ as the center of the universe and of the church and as crucial for human destiny. *We proclaim him*, declares the apostle Paul.

We come then finally to the pronoun *we*, and the maintenance of a mission: "*We* proclaim him."

In the Greek, this pronoun too is emphatic. It immediately distinguishes Paul and his fellow-preachers—Timothy and Epaphras (v. 7)—from those false teachers in Colossae who, by a curious mixture of Hebrew and Greek elements, spoke of mediators and mediation and promoted worship of angelic beings. Their religious syncretism greatly reduced the role of Christ and stripped him of preeminence. In a somewhat different way, current theological and philosophical and political outlooks do this in our own day. Jesus is mentioned; he has a place, though not first place and often not even an authentic place. Paul saw in all this a perversion of the gospel, and that is a warning to us.

Paul had become a minister of the gospel, a *diakonos* or "servant" charged with a message about Christ that he must get to the whole world.

I do not want to blur the uniqueness of that apostolic call and ministry in what I say next. But I would not have chosen this text were I unpersuaded that we, too, are somehow meshed into that same mission. Paul's primary reference in context is doubtless to himself as an apostle and to the faithful teachers that the apostles had trained or helped to preach that same gospel. Jesus had earlier instructed the disciples: "As the Father has sent me, I am sending you" (John 20:21). In B.F. Westcott's words, they were integrated into the redemptive covenant of the Godhead. What catastrophe if Christ had not come; what tragedy if the apostles had not gone, but had kept the message to themselves.

But we stand in the succession of witnesses, beginning with John the Baptist, who testify to the incarnate Son and orchestrate good news to the world. So the "we"—"*we* proclaim him"—comes in turn to include all Christians. If the "we" who preach Christ pertained only to the apostolic age, Christianity might well have perished with the first century. I cannot escape the conviction that the great apostle would wish to arch forward into our time and place not only the *him* and not only the *proclaiming* of the past but the urgency of our individual engagement, and that he would say something person-to-person, one-on-one about each of us being the lifeline in our time in some desperately important sense akin to his being the lifeline, along with Epaphras and Timothy, in the first century. It is imperative that we who are meshed to this mission, who are called to preserve and maintain it, make Paul's "we proclaim him" our very own.

Other bridges may intimidate us when first we venture them. The Colossian bridge is so awesome and overwhelming that it may leave us aghast as we try to proclaim Christ to our contemporaries. But the great apostle stirs us to action by his own example; he labored, he says, straining like an athlete with all the energies at his disposal. Surely the Olympic Games give us a continuing reminder of what that means. More than that, the Spirit of Christ, he says, was a power in him that quickened fulfillment of his mission: "To this end I labor, struggling with all his energy, which so powerfully works in me" (v. 29).

Take the wheel and drive over this bridge. See the world as Paul saw it, lost and desperately in need of the Savior. *We proclaim him!* The supremacy of Christ; the priority of preaching; the maintenance of a mission! May the Spirit of God make these realities our very own.

The Modern Importance of the Resurrection

What significance has the resurrection of Jesus of Nazareth from the dead for us today? Dare we shrug off that event much as our news-hardened twentieth century tends to reel and roll with whatever happens to make the morning headlines?

The teaching of the Risen Lord came from resurrection lips, from the other side of death, and holds absolute importance for his followers and for the whole human race.

Among the Risen Jesus' first exhortations to his disciples is, "Do not be afraid" (Matthew 28:10). He assures our anxiety-ridden generation that sin and evil and injustice will not have the last word, and that God's purpose will triumph over death itself. Behind whatever locked doors we may hide ourselves in fear of the future, Jesus strides through those very doors to offer personal peace to an anguished age: "Stop being afraid . . . Peace be with you."

Another admonition of the Risen Lord is to be empowered by the Holy Spirit. His disciples cannot cope in their own strength with world wickedness. In a world where atomic and nuclear power are commonplace, a needlessly unempowered church is a double embarrassment. We are to be superconquerors—not political tyrants but ethical and spiritual giants among the moral pygmies of our age. Christ stipulated the Holy Spirit as the supernatural source of our moral power in a society steeped in permissiveness.

A third word of the Risen Lord is the deputation to witness to the world. The Great Commission—"Go!"—fell from resurrection lips. It mandates us to proclaim Good News to all the nations and to baptize and instruct the unreached multitudes in the will and purpose of God.

These living words of the Risen Jesus still confront his followers with the exhortation: Don't be intimidated, but be empowered by the Spirit, and carry the gospel to the remotest edges of the earth.

More than that, Jesus' Easter morning resurrection publishes the uncompromising righteousness of God to all mankind. The only human nature God applauds and singularly promoted into the eternal future is that of Jesus Christ, the perfect Son of God. God has not raised from the dead Pontius Pilate or Herod or Caiaphas, who must wait their day; he has not even raised Augustine or Luther or Calvin or Wesley, not even Moses or John the Baptist or the apostle Paul, but Jesus only, Jesus whom the Father has exalted at his right hand. In the whole history of humanity, Jesus stands out as " *the* just and holy *one*"— the one, the only one. Jesus' resurrection bears witness to all the generations that one dramatic exception exists to the universal clutch of sin and death upon beleaguered mankind, and that singular exception is Jesus of Nazareth.

It is his human nature alone that God approves and commends going into the eternal future. Speak as we may at times of Christians as "little Jesuses," we are far less than that even at our best. Nobody but Jesus has marched into the world of death and defanged it, marched through it and left it in disarray, stripped away its sting and triumphed over it. The exclusivity of Jesus' resurrection speaks to all human beings of the supreme righteousness of God manifest in the Risen Redeemer.

The resurrection of the Crucified One attests another fact: Jesus' death was a voluntary act of self-giving love. A mother may die to give birth to a baby; a man may die for a friend; a compassionate, moral man may even die for a stranger; but sooner or later death would greet all of these, as it will all of us; it is inevitable. You and I have no inherent exemption from death. At best we do not long survive three score years and ten. Our deserved destiny would condemn us all forever to the final and irreversible grip of death. But when Scripture affirms that "Christ died for our sins," it speaks of the God-man who yielded himself voluntarily to death, of Jesus who said, "No one takes [my life] from me, but I lay it down of my own accord" (John 10:18). The resurrection shows that the crucified Lord of life experienced death as a sacrificial substitute, that he voluntarily bore a penalty undeserved by him and assumed in our stead, who truly deserved it. The Crucified One's resurrection is evidence that, in distinction from all the rest of us, Jesus Christ could not and cannot be holden in death, but went to the cross in our place, bearing our guilt and penalty in self-giving love.

The resurrection of Jesus of Nazareth is the crowning assurance that the gospel is no mere speculative philosophy or private perspective on life and reality. It involves historical redemptive acts and objectively revealed divine truths and commandments. The Christian gospel brings salvation to all who make it their own, writes the apostle Paul. And what is that gospel? It is the incomparable good news that "Christ died for our sins according to the Scriptures," that although he was buried, he was raised the third day and appeared (1 Corinthians 15:3-5a). Paul details the specifics: the Risen Christ appeared to Cephas, to the Twelve, and to many more—indeed, Paul seems almost to taunt the skeptics when he adds that the Risen Jesus appeared "to more than five hundred of the brothers at the same time" and then stressed that "most of whom are still living" (1 Corinthians 15:6).

We are not dealing with literary fiction and intellectual conjecture—with myths—when we speak of the incarnation, crucifixion, and resurrection of Jesus of Nazareth. The Resurrection confirms that Christianity is about God who is active in nature and in history, and in saving sinners who turn to him for grace. The Bible has as its climax the person of Jesus Christ—the centrality of his incarnation, crucifixion, and resurrection as the promised Messiah, who took on himself our human nature, lived a perfect life, died an atoning death, and rose in triumph over the tomb.

Another point that follows from Christ's resurrection bears on political realities, on the rulers of the nations. The last time you read of Pontius Pilate in the New Testament, two prominent Christians are begging the pagan Roman governor for the body of Jesus. We read about it in John's Gospel: "Later, Joseph of Arimathea asked Pilate for the body of Jesus. Now Joseph was a disciple of Jesus, but secretly because he feared the Jews. With Pilate's permission, he came and took the body away. He was accompanied by Nicodemus, the man who earlier had visited Jesus at night. Nicodemus brought a mixture of myrrh and aloes, about seventy-five pounds. Taking Jesus' body, the two of them wrapped it, with the spices, in strips of linen. This was in accordance with Jewish burial customs." (John 19:38-40). But nobody has to ask for the body of Jesus today. The next time world rulers and kings see the body of Jesus will be on that coming judgment day when all will bow the knee to the King of kings and Lord of lords. Khomeini will be there, and Mao Tse-Tung, and Adolph Hitler, and Gorbachev, and Botha, and Shamir, and Margaret Thatcher, and Ronald Reagan, too. The Risen Jesus will be the judge of all men and nations.

The fact of Jesus' resurrection has implications also for the great nonbiblical religions and their founders— Confucius, Buddha, Muhammad, and others—and for the originators of modern religious novelties like Mary Baker Eddy and Christian Science, Joseph Smith and Mormonism, Charles Taze Russell and Jehovah's Witnesses, and so on. Not many years ago in Chicago, evangelist Billy Graham was holding a citywide evangelistic meeting in Soldier Field. The Jesus People wanted to reach Chicago's inner city young people with a promotion less staid and more contemporary than dignified crusade advertising. In a popular television program at the time, viewers tried to distinguish a particular celebrity from two imposters. You recall the punch line: "Will the real so-and-so please stand up?" The Jesus People distributed a cartoon that showed several tombs holding the remains of founders of the great world religions. Underneath was the line: "Will the real Messiah please stand up?" Only one of those tombs was empty—the tomb of Jesus. The others were still in the grip of death. The Risen Jesus controls the sluicegates of eternity; the founders of nonbiblical religions will be answerable to him in the life to come.

It should give us no cause for glee that the rulers of this world and the founders of the nonbiblical religions will be gathered at the judgment throne of the risen Christ. The apostle Paul warned the Athenians that Jesus' resurrection serves advance notice that he will judge the whole world in righteousness, ourselves included. "[God] commands all people everywhere to repent," Paul proclaimed on Mars Hill, "for he has set a day when he will judge the world with justice by the man he has appointed. He has given proof of this to all men by raising him from the dead" (Acts 17:30ff.).

The resurrection of Jesus is the pledge also of the future resurrection of the whole human race. His "third day" resurrection as the God-man guarantees our future end-time resurrection, for Scripture says that he arose as the advance harvest of a universal resurrection. "Christ has indeed been raised from the dead, the firstfruits of those who have fallen asleep," writes Paul of one phase of that coming harvest involving "each in his own turn: Christ, the firstfruits; then, when he comes, those who belong to him" (1 Corinthians 15:20,23). Beyond that, Jesus himself warned, "a time is coming when all who are in their graves will hear his voice and come out—those who have done good will rise to live, and those who have done evil will rise to be condemned" (John 5:28f.).

Another consequence of Christ's resurrection is that the possibility of salvation remains open in this life even now to the most radical opponents of God and his Christ. To atheists and agnostics, to tyrants and terrorists, to the most monstrous persecutors and foes of the truth of God, Paul's experience of salvation on the Damascus Road is a reminder of the present possibility of a new beginning, a new life, a new destiny. Christ can take one not even deserving to be called an apostle, as Paul describes himself (1 Corinthians 15:9), and make a new creature, forgiven and redeemed and renewed, and on daily speaking terms with the Risen Lord. All the penitent, worldwide, remain within saving reach of the Risen Lord.

The resurrection of Jesus is not only a standing invitation to personal faith in the Risen Redeemer, but it is an incentive to service; it is a guarantee that our good deeds have eternal significance and worth. Paul may never have seen Jesus during his earthly ministry, but from the appearance of the Risen Jesus he received such motivation that he "worked harder than all of them" (1 Corinthians 15:10), even more than those who had walked the Palestinian byways with Jesus during the days of his flesh. We serve a Risen Lord who said, "All authority in heaven and on earth has been given to me. . . . And surely, I am with you always, to the very end of the age" (Matthew 28:18f.).

Christ's resurrection spurs the church not only to the evangelistic proclamation of personal salvation, but to the promotion of world justice. The victory over injustice and evil that Jesus won in his own conquest over sin and death he wishes to extend through the church, of which he has become the living and exalted head. The church is not simply to preach personal salvation, but is to publish the criteria by which Christ will judge the world and even now judges it, and to affirm God's interest in the whole person and the whole world. The church is to live as the new society within a rebellious world, and is to challenge and call humanity to authentic life and hope, and to exhibit what it means to live by the standards of the returning King. The resurrection therefore strips away all racial, national, economic, and cultural distinctions; it is not bounded by differences of color and culture, of race and rank. It reminds us that the God of the eternal future is the God of creation and redemption who discriminates not on the basis of pigment, but on the basis of justice and mercy, of purity and penitence.

Finally, the visible resurrection of Jesus is the pledge that Jesus will return personally and visibly to consummate his kingdom in triumphant power and glory. He came and left in person as the incarnate and crucified Logos; now he is the risen and returning Lord. The apostle John writes that when the Risen Jesus returns "every eye will see him, even those who pierced him" (Revelation 1:7). Remember the ascension morning testimony when the Risen Jesus returned to the Father and resumed the glory that was his before the world began: "This same Jesus, who has been taken from you into heaven, will come back in the same way you have seen him go into heaven" (Acts 1:11). We shall behold him—either as the Judge before whom mankind cowers, or as the Redeemer whose return the people of God cherish.

That Jesus is risen attests that his teaching has firm anchorage in eternity—that in Jesus, God has already welcomed to himself the one and only bearer of a sinless humanity, that Jesus was not holden of death but died voluntarily, that the gospel is not literary myth but is rooted in historical redemptive acts and in divinely revealed truth, that the rulers of the nations and founders of nonbiblical religions must yet appear at Jesus' throne, that the whole human race will be resurrected in the end-time, that salvation remains today an option even for persecutors like Saul of Tarsus, that our Christian service and dedication to good works has a guaranteed survival value, that the church of which the Risen Lord is head is to extend his victory over injustice and evil, and that Christ will return as King in power and glory to consummate his kingdom.

PART 3

WHERE ARE
THE PHYSICIANS?

Truths You Have Learned

*I*t is neither the best of times nor the worst of times. But it is a time when all the modern gods are sick and dying. The nations that long lusted after power are now terrified by it. Sex has played itself out for many who thought an infinity of it would be heaven on earth. The almighty dollar is falling like a burned-out star. It is a day made-to-order for sons of the prophets, for sons of the apostles, for Protestant Reformers, and for evangelical giants.

In 2 Timothy the apostle Paul writes to his son in the ministry about the truths "you have learned and have become convinced of " (2 Timothy 3:14). Allow me now to thrust upon you three matters that concerned the great apostle. Paul speaks of the *source* of these truths, the *scope* of these truths, and the *sequel* to these truths. I can do no better.

First, *the source of divine truth*. From his grandmother Lois and his mother Eunice, Timothy had first learned these truths. He had learned them in a spiritually pluralistic home, one with a mixed marriage. Yet somebody had faithfully conveyed

---

Commencement address delivered at Biola University, La Mirada, California, 9 May 1982.

the truth of the gospel that Paul now expected Timothy to share with others.

The ultimate source of this divine wisdom was neither Timothy's mother nor his grandmother. It was the living God specially made known in Christ and in scripturally-given revelation. "From infancy," writes Paul, "you have known the holy Scriptures, which are able to make you wise for salvation through faith in Christ Jesus" (3:15).

The fountain of this wisdom, Paul emphasizes, is God: "All Scripture is God-breathed" (3:16), he writes. In Scripture the living God records his word, the divinely inspired prophets and divinely inspired apostles convey to man a transcendently given truth of God. When E. F. Hutton speaks, so the commercial runs, people listen. But E. F. Hutton can be wrong. When theologians speak, students may listen, but their teachers are not infallible. But the God of the Bible does not traffic in error, in falsehood and fabrication. When God speaks, worlds come into being, stars move in their courses, sinners are reborn, nations rise and fall, prophets and apostles pen his word.

The apostle Paul declares Scripture in its entirety—every and all Scripture—to be divinely inspired. God is the source of this truth.

Second, *the sequel to divine truth*. You have often heard it said that "ideas have consequences." They do indeed, for good or ill. Think of the bitter consequences that have befallen our century because of Nazi ideology, Marxist ideology, Maoist ideology. But God's truth too has its sequel, its incomparable sequel. Our appropriation or nonappropriation of it shapes our lives on earth and will shape our eternal destiny. "Christ rose from the dead," writes Paul, therefore the rest of us will be raised also, some to condemnation and some to life eternal.

"Continue in what you have learned and have become convinced of," writes Paul. Upon that continuance may well depend the spiritual and moral fortunes of our unsteady nation. "Keep on believing," says the Living Bible, "Keep to what you have been taught," says the Jerusalem Bible. But the apostle is not asking us merely to hold out individually against the tide of the times. "Stand by" the truths you have learned—as the New English Bible puts it—doesn't imply that we who know God's truth are, like Peter, to be mere bystanders where the fire burns, secret disciples, believing privately so none will know our loyalties and as if Jesus and his mandate were not our life priorities. "Stand by" doesn't mean "to be a bystander." The stately King James, the Revised Standard, and the New International versions all join in exhorting us to "continue" in those truths. "Go on steadily in those things," echoes Phillips. For the goal of revealed truth is that the man of God may be thoroughly equipped for every good work (3:17). Not half equipped for some good works, but thoroughly equipped for every good work.

To be sure, on many current issues we evangelicals have no better information than do contemporary humanists, and on some issues we and they alike have far less knowledge than does a small cadre of informed technicians. Yet if we do what Scripture expressly enjoins, we shall address the good works that God stipulates and not concentrate on debatable matters while neglecting what God specifically commands. In a world that has lost its way we can, if powered by the Holy Spirit, strive in love to fulfill the divine imperatives on which a stable society depends. Let it be said that in a time of intellectual confusion and moral relativism, we who cherish the Bible hold together in an exemplary way both the word of God and the works of God.

The apostle Paul tells us that all Scripture is profitable. A profit-oriented society like ours, one would think, would perk up its ears when Paul mentions the fourfold profitability of Scripture: Scripture is profitable, the apostle says, for teaching the truth, for refuting error, for correction, and for training in right living. Millions upon millions of people would be lifted above life that is bitter and bewildering if their minds and deeds were shaped by the revealed truth of God. In our materially-minded world, life's greatest profitability still lies in heeding what the Bible teaches.

Paul assumes that we are not simply parroting the velvet vocabulary of a few memorable lectures, but rather that we are thoroughly convinced of certain truths, that these great convictions have become the very pulsebeat and bloodflow of our lives, and that we are ready to put body and soul on the lifeline of our great technological civilization in what may well be its twilight hours. Paul assumes that we are messengers of hope to a condemned generation in need of new life, which otherwise faces an ignominious death. If there is to be good news in our time, the people of God must herald it. If there is to be moral power—sexual integrity, marital fidelity, and vocational responsibility—the people of God must exhibit it. If there is durable meaning in life, the people of God must identify it. If there is holy joy and peace in an age that devalues the spiritual virtues, then God's people must show neighbor-love and love of God to be alive in the community of man.

All around us the world sees the dread consequences of atheism, skepticism, doubt, and unbelief; let the sequel of our commitment to the truth of revelation be a New Society of twice-born men and women whose way of life truly approximates the Kingdom of God, one that offers hope to a multitude for whom life has turned sour and embittered, and that takes its stand for human rights and for religious freedom in an age of totalitarian tyrants. For some that may spell martyrdom; for others, imprisonment; for yet others, intense persecution. For all of us it means—whatever may be our vocation—being living epistles of God known and read by our fellowmen.

Finally, having spoken of the source and the sequel of divine truth, let me now speak of *the scope of God's revealed truth*. Scripture addresses the great problems of our time and the perplexities of all the ages of man.

What many American contemporaries do not know, you and I know very well: that material components do not constitute the ultimately real world; that man is not merely an animal in a chance-strewn cosmos; that truth is not subject to revision as are the airline schedules; that the good and the true cannot be reduced to whatever Hollywood and Madison Avenue momentarily approve, or to whatever culture-ridden sociologists and secular humanists commend. You know that man does not ultimately control the universe and that he will not have the last word. You know that a transcendent world exists, one not comprised of space-time relativities but rather one that governs eternal destinies as all mankind moves toward an inescapable life to come.

Even the classical Greek philosophers, pagans though they were, unfamiliar with Scripture though they were, championed the primacy of an eternal, supernatural world. They taught of man's superiority over the animals in view of his rational and moral nature and believed in the ultimacy and finality of truth and the good. Plato and Aristotle stressed all these tenets, even though they did not have the Bible in whole or in part, but had only God's universal revelation in common with other sinners (who in their reception of it manipulate and distort that revelation). It invites terrible judgment upon the modern mindset that multitudes of our contemporaries do not affirm these verities.

In the coming judgment of modern unbelief, the ancient pagan Greeks will rise to witness against the great modern learning centers of Europe and the Anglo-Saxon West wherever our century sweeps away the supernatural, wherever it limits reality to the grid of empirical observation, wherever it sucks the whole of existence into the natural sciences, wherever it refers all the complex forms of life to natural evolution and natural selection and chance variation in a cosmic lottery, wherever it reduces the ultimate world to impersonal processes and events and dismisses mind and personality and values as fate and accidental emergents in the flux of things. Even Plato and Aristotle had a grander vision of truth and of the good than have towering twentieth century thinkers like John Dewey and B. F. Skinner. The scientism that would bring everything under human control already in principle arbitrarily eclipses the transcendent eternal world to which man is answerable and upon which the cosmos even now depends. In the coming judgment of men and nations, even the pagan intellectuals of ancient Greece and Rome will rise to judge the naturalistic bias that today grips so much of Western thought and pervades so much of American liberal learning. We should not much compliment ourselves that, along with the classic Greek sages, we at least affirm these things. That these ancient pagan principles far excel even the naturalism, humanism, and relativism of our present age indicates how far Western civilization has sunk into the mires of antisupernaturalism, and how preoccupied our generation is with changing space-time relativities.

Yet, for all their insights, the classic Greek and Roman philosophers should give the Christian task force little consolation. Use a bit of historical imagination, if you will, even of poetical imagination. Suppose that you and I, and Plato and Aristotle, and the apostles Paul and Peter and John were gathered here among this throng, and that you were speaking rather than I. Suppose you had trumpeted all the truths we have heard—about the ultimately real spiritual world, about a future destiny of man in the age to come, about the unchanging character of truth and the good. Who do you think would applaud? Who, other than pagan Greeks and Romans? Jews and Christians, I submit, would keep a stony silence, or with the apostle Paul would invite us to Mars Hill. The tenets we have outlined—the reality of the supernatural, man's superiority over other mammals, the fixed character of truth and the good, and the surety of immortality—were not only the routine assumptions of ancient paganism, but also were premises that secular philosophers developed in a perversely nonbiblical way, one to which the early Christians from the first proclaimed an alternative. The Greek and Roman emphases were in fact enthusiastically shared by virtually all the modernist rationalists, *against* whom evangelical Christians in the forepart of this century had to wage theological battle.

Between philosophical idealism and speculative theism on the one hand and authentic biblical theology on the other, there is a night and day difference like that between sunset and high noon. Those secular philosophers in ancient and modern times, even if they repudiated naturalism, shared in the human revolt against the one living God and contributed to a distortion of divine revelation.

It is the Bible that tells mankind of the living, sovereign Creator who has made the universe out of nothing. *It is the Bible* that tells us that God fashioned man in his holy image for spiritual fellowship. *It is the Bible* that affirms man's universal sinfulness in Adam and the need of redemptive grace that God alone can offer, a salvation we do not merit and cannot by our works provide. *It is the Bible* that makes known the God of Covenant, who chooses Abraham's seed, rescues the Israelites from Egyptian bondage, and makes them his theocratic people. *It is the Bible* that discloses God's messianic promises and unveils Jesus of Nazareth as incarnate deity. *It is the Bible* that declares Christ's virgin birth, sinless life, substitutionary death, bodily resurrection, headship of the church, and priestly ministry. And *it is the Bible* that declares Christ's imminent return to judge men and nations.

Stand by the truths you have learned; continue in them! Let them be your life; share them with a beleaguered and bewildered age. In this doomsday generation, speak them loud to this wayward world. Live as those who know the Creator Redeemer God, the God of grace and glory who in that great and final homecoming of his people will welcome us as those who do not misperceive the Way, the Truth, or the Life.

Politics and the Church

*T*he longer I observe the historical development of two types of totalitarianism in the modern world, the more grateful I am for our democratic alternative. Islam and the Islamic world consider Muslim religion and politics inseparable; the only question is the identity of Muhammad's successor and ruler of the Muslim community. The communist Soviet Union, by contrast, espouses the absolute separation of church and state.

The New Testament, which is the Christian church's charter religious document, declares both church and civil government to be divinely willed instrumentalities with distinct powers, spheres, and purposes under God. The Constitution, the charter political document of the United States, protects the free exercise of religion while it excludes the official establishment of religion.

While the First Amendment seeks to avoid the political establishment of a national religion or denomination, it does not seek to advance the irrelevance of religion or to promote irreligion. The Declaration of Independence, in fact, recognized that human rights have a theistic basis.

Delivered to a panel of The Institute on Religion and Democracy, 10 December 1984, in Washington, D.C.

The wall between church and state in America is a serpentine wall, not a rigid and strictly exclusive barrier. The interaction between church and state, or state and church, is what has led to the questions: Does politics belong in the church? Does the church belong in politics?

The meaning of the term *church* is not self-evident, and the term *politics* or notion of political engagement also covers a multitude of virtues, vices and ambiguities. By *church* is now often meant (1) a building used for Christian religious purposes; (2) a locally organized congregation or body of members; (3) a major branch of Christendom; (4) a denomination; (5) a hierarchy or duly constituted leadership that speaks authoritatively for a church constituency or that professes so to speak. The church may therefore be vulnerable to politicization at different levels.

So, too, *politics* has a multilevel meaning. It embraces governmental institutions, political principles, party organizations and platforms, and political methods and strategy.

Evangelicals were stigmatized from 1950 to 1970 as insisting that religion and politics are alien spheres. This misrepresentation served the cause of nonevangelical ecumenists and critics more than it served the cause of truth or accorded with history. The emphasis "the church should not meddle in politics" held a special meaning acquired in a historical context in which ecumenical hierarchies claimed to speak as the church, routinely championed leftist social theories as gospel truth, and imputed a divine aura to particular programs and legislation without logically deriving them from scriptural principles. What ecumenical political involvement implied was a program of nonsupernatural social redemption with discernible Marxist tendencies, and the consequent neglect of evangelism and missions as an outmoded task.

When in the late seventies evangelicals aggressively returned to the political arena, they did not do so—contrary to their critics—by way of an unprecedented American religious incursion into politics. Nor was it simply a matter of duplicating on the right what ecumenists had been doing on the left. Rather, it was in line with public involvement of eighteenth century

Revolutionary clergy who preached "liberty," of nineteenth century involvement in the abolition movement, and of early twentieth century involvement in the Prohibition movement; it was in line, moreover, with my own plea in *The Uneasy Conscience of Modern Fundamentalism* at midcentury that public affairs not be left to nonevangelical political forces. *Christianity Today* recognized from its beginnings the importance of social as well as personal ethics and of the application of biblical principles to the whole sociocultural arena, even if its energies were often exhausted in challenging ecumenical conceptions.

Our topic implies that both the church and the state may be the offending partner in the matter of incursion into each other's spheres.

Without doubt, it was recent governmental incursion into the ecclesiastical realm, even more than long-smoldering reaction to the ecumenical front or a conscious formulation of a comprehensive social and political philosophy, that stirred the evangelical right to bold political engagement. The 1973 Supreme Court decision on federal funding of abortion, the 1978 Internal Revenue Service proposal to impose racial tests on Christian schools, and other disputed federal activities spurred evangelicals to political response. The emergence of the electronic church provided telecasters Jerry Falwell, Pat Robertson, and others a wide opportunity to rally and mobilize evangelical constituencies for political guidance and nurtured the growth of Christian Voice, Moral Majority, and other movements.

The encroachment of government into the church is more subtle than many religious leaders suspect. This naivete is due in part to their welcoming media exposure that enhances personal popularity and organizational visibility. Political incumbents and candidates routinely view church and synagogue as important political constituencies and create a public impression of sympathetic identification by aptly-phrased convention addresses and by posing with ecclesiastical leaders whose flocks misread this association in terms of special access and private influence. The church has reason to beware of Caesar bearing pious political rhetoric.

Glaring politicization of the church was evident in the recent use of black churches, not only as voting registration centers, but also for promotion in church services of a particular candidate and for the direct solicitation of offerings for political campaigns. Only a biased media could have connected the discussion of ecclesiastical politicization with the activity of the religious right, while ignoring such direct deployment of churches by the religious left, or indulging it as only a matter of campaign style or black culture.

Does the church belong in politics? Insofar as it owns land and buildings, the church clearly has civic obligations and should render to Caesar what is properly Caesar's. As an institution grounded on a divine disclosure of truth and morality, moreover, the church is mandated to proclaim publicly the revealed principles by which Christ the King of kings will ultimately judge nations and states and does so even now. The church as such must also stimulate members to apply scriptural principles with sound reason and in good conscience to current political concerns, in quest of preferred policies and programs promoting justice and peace. Since God wills the state as an instrumentality for preserving justice and restraining disorder, the church should urge members to engage in political affairs to their utmost competence and ability, to vote faithfully and intelligently, to engage in the political process at all levels, and to seek and hold public office. The church is not, however, to use the mechanisms of government to legally impose upon society at large her theological commitments.

The church must increasingly clarify when obedience to God requires disobedience to the state and, no less, when disobedience to the state constitutes disobedience to God. Politically enhancing media coverage offers a ready temptation to engage unlawfully on the domestic scene in acts of protest against immoral policies abroad. In a world in which deliberate violation, however well-intentioned, readily encourages massive disregard for law, and even invites lawless terrorism if lesser means fail to achieve one's ends, the refusal to seek change through duly constituted legal processes may be civilizationally costly. The church knows that God is the transcendent source and sanction of law, and the clergy especially ought to know that man is not above it in the absence of a clear and scriptural mandate for civil disobedience.

No ecclesiastical hierarchy speaks authoritatively for evangelical Christians, who seek to bring themselves directly under the Bible. Evangelicals countered the atheistic humanist invasion of American political philosophy by affirming scripturally-grounded values. When this was deplored as an attempt to impose Judeo-Christian religion upon a pluralistic society, Moral Majority insisted that it was not a theological movement. Its political strength lay in the insistence that public policy must not erode civilizational values.

The religious right, nonetheless, accelerated fears of an imposition of sectarian morality in the political arena. This anxiety was deliberately escalated by secular humanists who assume that all ethical norms and prescriptions are man-made, experimental, and ever-changing. As the evangelical right blended morality and politics, the liberal left insisted that morality and politics not be confused. For the left, tolerance became so much the supreme good that any and all absolutes (other than tolerance) bore the specter of totalitarian imposition by a fundamentalist Khomeini.

There was, however, another facet to the debate. Some evangelicals, whose concern for moral absolutes is commendable, continued to speak of America in terms of an ideal theocracy or christocracy in political affairs. The American charter political documents, to be sure, do not speak of a value-neutrality or of a self-sustaining morality.

At least two things in a pluralistic society now remain for evangelicals to clarify : how to encapsulate in legislation moral values that are not merely sectarian, but also constitute the ethical foundation of a viable state; and to identify the political rhetoric most appropriate to a republic in which civil government is the arbiter of neither metaphysical nor theological concerns.

God's Press Corps in the Cultural Crossfire

I write to journalists under appointment to the King: that, at least, is how I view evangelical journalism. My early roots were in secular newspaperwork. When I became a Christian and was called to ministry, I felt that to return to journalism would betray my calling. But my theological training soon taught me that "all things are Christ's" and that, under Christ, they are mine for service and witness wherever I am—in the church, in the editorial room, or on campus.

We live in a darkening civilization in which worldlings seek to divide Christ's garments among them. Lebanon is but one of many tragic symbols of secular history—Muslims and Israelis at each other's throats while Christians, caught in the middle, perish in a face-off between the world's superpowers. Evangelicals are persecuted in atheistic Russia and much of eastern Europe, are beleaguered in China, prohibited from building churches in Saudi Arabia, arrested for distributing literature in Turkey, and no less tragic, are often vilified in the United States.

This address was given at the keynote banquet of the 36th annual Evangelical Press Association convention on Monday night, 2 May 1984, at Key Bridge Marriott in Rosslyn, Arlington, Virginia.

121

Too few statesmen challenge world leaders who pledge religious liberty on paper but hamper it in public. Many diplomats are baffled by the political pregnancy of religious beliefs: they seem blind to the fact that Muslims have always relied on the sword and not on persuasion to widen Koranic world power, and they fail to see how urgently America needs, herself, to return to the God of all nations. It is incongruous, indeed, that communist leaders, atheist though they be, take the God of the Bible seriously enough to penalize believers, while many free world spokesmen ignore the deity as if he were a public nuisance.

As secular powers tighten their grip and entrench themselves ever more fully, it is our duty as Christian writers to illumine the credibility and claims of biblical Christianity for all mankind. The Bible draws an ultimately decisive line in history not between communist world and free world, nor even between Israelis and Muslims, but between the regenerate church and the unregenerate world. Clarifying that line, pressing its implications upon our generation, is the primary duty of evangelical journalism.

In elaborating on that sense of duty, I may perhaps overwork the word and even the syllable, *press*. Be that as it may, I want to speak now, in the context of the evangelical press, of *depression* and of *expression*. To do this requires a certain veiled omniscience, of course, and my credentials are therefore less than impeccable. But perhaps we can at least get a fix on evangelical journalism and perchance help our cause a bit.

First, the bad news: evangelical depression. Who knows? You and I may be living in the very last generation of religious publications. According to some technologists, computers that avoid publishing delays and mailing costs will, sooner or later, doom newspapers and magazines to the graveyard. In my opinion, books—although not all books—have an assured future, and best of all, the Book of books. But something is surely in the wind when Oxford University Press puts an eighty-nine dollar retail price on a 410-page volume of miscellaneous works by John Bunyan. We cannot take the future for granted.

In any case, God's press corps is stationed here and now in the present cultural crossfire. We need, therefore, to ask ourselves some penetrating questions. For what does the evangelical press really count in this confused world? Who trembles when God goes to press? Who's afraid of the E.P.A.? Are we merely closet opinion-makers? Are we publicly quoted only when we would rather not be—indeed, embarrassed if we are quoted? Does what we say recognizably echo the Word of God? Or is what we say simply one statement among many in a pluralistic society? Worse yet, is what we say crafted to give our potential market audience only what it wants to hear?

What went wrong with "the year of the evangelical"? What skewed those presumptuous prophecies of evangelical awakening in America? Some well-traveled spokesmen saw no warning for us in the cultural drift across the Atlantic. In Scotland, the land of John Knox, for example, 60 percent of the people now lack even a formal connection with Christian churches, and in church colleges lecturers are not hard to find who do not even attend religious services. Surely here on Billy Graham's turf and Bill Bright's and Oral Roberts's and Jerry Falwell's, in the land of *Christianity Today* and Fuller Seminary, of the 700 Club and the P.T.L. network and Robert Schuller's Crystal Cathedral, would not brilliant parachurch maneuvering and evangelical entrepreneurship forestall any such drastic decline as on the Continent and in Britain, and instead usher in a new Reformation, a new evangelical awakening? What went wrong?

What lies ahead for us—not a generation hence but right now—for an evangelical enterprise whose subsurface rivalries and breakaway movements continue to frustrate any overall comprehensive thrust? What awaits a movement if its idolized spokesmen are given more to polemics than to theological precision, more to public relations or to national image than to powerful convictions, more to team patriotism than to creative vision, more to statistics than to substance? We cried out against the merely quantitative measurement of success in Vietnam in terms of body count, yet we judge the triumph of our colleges

and seminaries and evangelistic crusades and religious publications by the number of scalps of students, spectators, or subscribers they display. Evangelical empire-builders openly hail
Mr. Reagan's spiritual and moral leadership, yet when the
gifted incumbent gifts a gifted pope with the gift of a papal am-
bassador for political advantage, do these same empire-builders
remain silent because they too are indebted to the White House
for personal and organizational visibility? Do the trappings of
power compromise us?

Does our computerized piety lack potency for evangelical
revival? Are the boasts we make compatible with our resources?
If we add up all the claims implicit in evangelical promotion,
would not the whole world recently have been converted twice
over, and would not all the dilemmas of our secular society already have been solved, except perhaps for a few mop-up operations before the looming millennium arrives? Haven't we all
been exposed to promotional panaceas (*be our guest at a free
dinner!*) that dangle the prospect of overnight utopia akin to the
instant gratification our age expects from glamour stocks
(*"Thank you, Paine Webber"*), or from miracle medicines that
work on television almost before one swallows them? Yet annual reports of evangelical causes promising to reshape the
planet often highlight not reliable flesh-and-blood statistics of
spiritual conquest, but rather plaintive pleas for funds to avoid
cash flow problems, nagging deficits, or even bankruptcy. What
penalties must any enterprise pay for exaggerating successes
and glossing over weaknesses?

Some observers estimate that 70 percent of the U.S. population remains unchurched and insist we are not as much removed from European heathenism as evangelical promotion
implies. The commercial trivialization of the West's sacred
heritage meanwhile continues apace. A television commercial
cloaks in medieval liturgy the "miraculous" performance of
Xerox copy machines, and a full-page Dictaphone Corporation
advertisement twists A.D. to mean not Anno Domini but "after
Dictaphone." The Italian sportswear manufacturer Mauritzio
Vitala promotes Jesus Jeans by distorting the Sinai command-

ment into "Thou shalt have no other jeans before me." Winston Churchill's great speeches are deployed to sell McDonald's chicken nuggets. During the 1983 Year of the Bible, eight major American corporations declined to sponsor a series of telecasts when media analysts decided that the Bible on film has no market value to our national viewing audience.

Shall we simply resign ourselves to humanist corruption of the mass media, to a largely anticognitive culture transmitted by radio and television and by much of the secular print media? Do the profaners have air rights to use foul obscenities on network programs? Should we leave, unchallenged, soap operas that imply that marriage is irrelevant to intercourse or to bearing children and that the family has little if any crucial structural role in society? Must viewers tune their sets to a hedonistic response zone, reserved for emotional exhilaration rather than for intellectual engagement, and directed more to orgasmic than cerebral activity, geared largely to the physical exploitation of eighteen- to thirty-four-year-old women?

Some discriminating contemporaries are turning to books instead of to television for learning and entertainment, and for good reason. Yet we must strenuously resist the notion that television is inherently evil. The church would have made a costly mistake had it shunned the printing press because it brought new powers of diffusion to evil as well as to good. The media do from time to time irrigate the spiritual lethargy of contemporary life. We have yet to realize how much their larger failure to do so may result from our own inertia.

There are those who would exploit even this secular mass market religiously, as if to say that when done in the name of religion nothing can be unethical, no matter how much one skims the truth (*"God told me to write you"* [this computerized correspondence]; *"send $20 right away or we must stop broadcasting"*). Is it truthful, is it spiritually decent to rerun funding appeals long after a specifically-indicated financial crisis has passed? And what about leaders whose lifestyles do violence to donors' expectations, not to mention God's expectations?

Has evangelical witness reached a monotonous plateau?

Have we come out of the ghetto into the culture mainly to preen ourselves in an increasingly immoral age? Can the church somehow break out of entrapment in the media culture? Do local congregations any longer yearn to be renewed in spiritual and ethical priorities? Are we now faced by a loss of momentum and a costly fallaway, perhaps even by the deadly final apostasy? Is America headed for a crumbling of her once-magnificent evangelical institutions and influences? Is the nation morally and spiritually doomed by the cultural crossfire? Has the preached Word of God any future in a society which, unlike that nurtured on Calvin's *Institutes,* is now fortunate to be confronted simply by "Four Things God Wants You to Know"?

Where today might a Jonathan Edwards rise to the presidency of Princeton, or a Timothy Dwight to the presidency of Yale, in a context of convictions that leaves in midair almost all that some evangelicals work for by way of an intellectual and theological renaissance? Many sons and daughters from evangelical homes and churches—more than you think—are unable to articulate their faith in the dechristianized university world. What help would most religious television programs offer them? Are not some of the most intellectual religious programs exasperatingly simplistic? "Get ready," a secular journalist told me recently, "for the Christian anchorman who will momentarily switch us to Jerusalem for a 'thirty second wrap-up' of the Second Coming."

Have we reached such an interim of intellectual sterility that publishers of religious books herald potboilers that specially cater to the pitch-it-low mentality? The romantic fiction some publishers currently commend because it stands on the side of evangelical morality in an immoral age may in fact be finally judged as a type of literary decadence if its disclosure of human character is too depthless and if it too feebly grapples modern life as it is. A mere recital of the ills of contemporary society, which one escapes in spiritual isolation with a devout mate, will not join battle with moderns who hurl themselves against the truth and strip conscience of basic biblical convictions.

Enough of evangelical depression; let us turn now to evangelical expression. We need editors who speak critically not only of the secular press but self-critically of evangelical ambiguities, hesitancies, and compromises. As I see it, the ultimate justification of an evangelical press is the illumination of God's Word and of its demands upon our generation. While a secular press may appoint itself an investigating and prosecuting agency, and even arrogate to itself the role of supreme court in society, an evangelical press is always under divine answerability. Nothing in the Bible requires that religious magazines publish on slick paper to inform pastors how to double their income as door-to-door salesmen, or to publicize spicy details about some disreputable religious leader's dalliance with his secretary, or even merely to entertain the hungry people of God with the clever warping and woofing of words.

Secular society is beginning to run away from us and we must overtake it. While purists have been asking how to seal off the church from the world, the world seems increasingly bent on sealing itself off from us. Raw naturalists and radical humanists do not in fact outnumber us, yet for all that, they often outmaneuver and outwit us. They lampoon a moral majority by impaling it on some single flaw, make a virtue out of their own association with some dissenting and even immoral minority, and thrive on publicity that spotlights their rejection of orthodoxy. They debunk the Bible as an establishment text chained to the status quo, a book that purportedly promotes male superiority and advocates sexual inhibition; one wonders how long it is since they have read it. Orwell's *1984* envisioned evangelicals and fundamentalists and orthodox Jews as strong and growing. Secular liberals, however, picture religious conservatives only in terms of Islamic violence and of a devotion to mythical absolutes. Religious liberals are more dedicated to nongender pronouns for God and Christ than to revealed propositions about supernatural theism, and they twist Scripture to condone homosexuality and to promote Marxism.

Who can doubt that new dimensions of shamelessness permeate modern society and that its horizons of licentiousness are reminiscent of pre-Christian paganism? A vocal vanguard vilifies the very norms of civilization; marriage it decries as bondage, sexual lust it defends as freedom. The biblical Elohim it classifies with the Loch Ness monster; references to God it views as escapist or as life-threatening. Acquisition of wealth becomes life's chief end and covetousness a cardinal virtue.

The liberal intellectual elite is self-assured that whatever future religion may have, it will not be in the form of biblical theism. Many regard religion as an epiphenomenal excrescence, one best outgrown in the interest of skepticism. The modern university, Robert Bellah notes, tends to relativize traditional world views by screening all basic premises through contemporary thought categories.[1]

The media reflect and parade naturalistic prejudices with little compunction to give equal time to theistic alternatives. To a global audience estimated at 140 million, Carl Sagan's television series *Cosmos* carried its humanistic bias against Judeo-Christian theism. Rejecting divine creation, it presented instead an all-embracing evolution as fact rather than theory.[2] If this view is taken seriously and man is but a cosmic freak, then death's present anteroom can lead only to inevitable nonbeing.

Has this revolt against Judeo-Christian principles reached such depths that, despite our crowded evangelical colleges and seminaries and growing evangelical churches, the evangelical place in American society has been forever altered? Is any deep spiritual awakening likely under present conditions: the clutch of secular humanism on our culture—on the media, on public education, and on the political arena; evangelical forces split into competing groups contending for prominence and preeminence; fundamentalism reorganizing for a takeover of conservative influence, yet ever spoiling for a fight on single-issue concerns; the rise among conservatives of rival theological journals, study groups, news letters, briefing conferences. Many of these efforts try to give the impression of some new moderating theological consensus or social emphasis. What they largely reflect, however, is a continuity of informal control over interlocking groups, groups that usually operate without power to represent fixed or official bodies but that give a surface impression of significant momentum. Over and above a few sessions of hoopla and pizzazz, stimulated by secular techniques for promotion, growth, and funding, how much promise does all this really hold for advancing the Kingdom of God and reshaping contemporary culture? We may think of ourselves as a brilliantly glowing beacon in the darkening world; can it be that God sees us, however, as but the stub of a sputtering candle on a planet desperately needing illumination?

What does it mean that evangelical evangelism records most of its successes today not by the evangelization of secular society, but on the margin of the already existing churches? Church growth philosophy normalizes this pursuit of internal additions mainly within the circle of immediate family friends—and who would gainsay its insight? But such spiritual expansion within already entrenched circles tends mostly to invigorate established churches and not to challenge communities and to renew cities.

Our nation now owns the highest divorce rate in the world. More than a million premarital teenage pregnancies occur annually, and Washington, D.C., has one of the nation's worst records in this regard. Does the District of Columbia really deserve national respect while over 56 percent of its reported births are to unmarried women?

Multitudes today live in sensual overdrive; so-called love is cheapened into a series of one-night stands devoured like so much junk food. Some practitioners, to be sure, are wearying of sex in the shadows; being unwanted except for the moment has shaped a painful epidemic of loneliness. Women who said "no" only because they feared pregnancy or communicable disease are discovering that sexual safeguards include more than abortion, namely, the far profounder perimeters of ethics and integrity. More and more get-with-it women now see that the sexual revolution has defrauded them. They long for interpersonal sensitivity and a recovery of moral sentiment.

A recent Gallup poll shows that despite the paganizing tide, some 46 percent of the adults in the United States are still likely to attend church or synagogue in a single week. Many in our decade therefore live only a doorstep from God's house, even if their neighbors may keep the deity at greater distance. What does this imply for evangelical access and impress? Are we too much concerned with a circus bandwagon of contemporary fads? What bearing have second-level, energy-depleting controversies such as fundamentalists and evangelicals derogating each other, conservative seminaries debating scriptural reliability, political activists condemning a lethargic church? Have we so blurred the priority of penetrating the nonevangelical multitude that other preoccupations turn the evangelical community inward upon itself? Are we impoverished by a loss of leadership in the world of ideas and in the arena of action?

Evangelism has financial and spiritual enthusiasm, but evangelism in and of itself cannot kindle the searing flame of contemporary cultural conviction. The evangelical impact continues to broaden, but it is diversifying more than it is deepening. Evangelism is being done not by the denominations as much as by individuals and parachurch enterprises.

The ecumenical pluralism of recent church history failed to build a world church; it actually lost more believers than it enlisted pagans. Although ecumenical financial reserves are substantial, ecumenism now pleads for funds more subtly but almost as energetically as do the electronic evangelists. Neither doctrinal diminution nor radical social action nor corporate worship that dwarfs precise creedal commitments has won the enthusiasm of ecumenical constituencies. Yet just when some Catholic churchmen are waiting for noncatholic ecumenism to expire, and when some ecumenical ecclesiasts think it time to post Luther-like reforming theses on doors in Geneva and New York, it is remarkable that some evangelicals on the political left, disenchanted with what passes for evangelical unity, now hail this same neo-Protestant ecumenism as the brightest hope for ecclesiastical renewal. What does it mean that while many evangelical leaders are excluded from the official councils of their churches, a second echelon of evangelicals courts ecumenical acclaim not for its apostolic heritage but for its political and social agenda?

Meanwhile, modern man in a confused pluralistic society is reaching for more and more religious options. People who stand for nothing, it seems, will fall for anything; the cults are having a heyday. The theory that a tolerant twentieth century mind should consider no theology and no religion false is as fallacious as metaphysical theory can be. We are doomed if we accept the notion that a truly educated person no longer needs to be knowledgeable in ethics, philosophy, or theology, or that these disciplines are less important than what we now call science. Humanists may insist that there is nothing of intellectual importance beyond what the modern mind can validate by empirical observation. But anyone who spends much time on today's campuses knows that the argument most students mount against belief in God is not a logical syllogism, but the complaint that the admission of deity would stifle weekend carousing and cavorting.

Our optimism lies in this, that scriptural imperatives retain their ultimacy in history. If we ourselves had to guarantee the future of our planet or the survival of the church, we might well be discouraged; but thank God, their foundation is Christ crucified and risen. God's purpose and providence and governance of history is the sheet anchor of Christian conviction. The forces that can defeat us are neither embedded in history nor grounded in nature nor eschatologically secure; they are contained within ourselves, in a misplaced confidence in our own abilities, in evangelical superstars or in the evangelical movement per se, and in a halting trust in the God of creation, providence, redemption, and judgment. Yet despite our misgivings about the future of evangelicalism, almost every observer of contemporary religious trends concedes that the permanent element in twentieth century religion in the United States is likely to be something doctrinally akin to present day evangelical-fundamentalist views. For the people of the Book the outcome need not be in doubt.

Without a return to fixed truth and shared values, no shift of emphasis in modern life will count for much, either in politics or anywhere else. The crisis of our culture is more fundamentally theological and ethical than political. Without a basic change of spiritual and moral condition, our nation is imperiled. To be sure, a recovery of Christianity and of a good society will not of itself guarantee permanent survival either of the West as a whole or even of America, nor should survival of the West as we now know it be the prime Christian objective. But such a recovery would at least renew vital fellowship with the Lord of history and with the unending God of all ends.

Immigrants have come from many lands looking to us for a viable alternative to personal despair. Some are disillusioned by the Asian suppression of selfhood in search of nirvana or of some transpersonal mystical core. Some Orientals glad to escape their history-eroding religions are astonished that some Americans now embrace these; they are equally stunned by the secular Western search for self-fulfillment through assertive egoism. Many immigrants are reaching not for bread alone but for moral reinforcement, for spiritual life, and for soul food. While our technological civilization may be bent on self-destruction, masses of humans still long for a personal faith.

If evangelical religion does not make sense of human existence and survival, if it provides no coherent hope for society, secular myths will preempt this role. As in pre-Christian antiquity, a mood of melancholy—a questioning of the worth of personal survival—is falling once again over human history. Every year twenty-seven thousand persons in the United States take their lives, and the suicide rate is now highest among young adults between fifteen and twenty-nine, higher among females than among males. Recent social studies link suicide less with unemployment than with church dropout. If churches fail to impress biblical alternatives on our age, if nothing in life is worth living for, then people will die for and with false prophets like those of Jonestown.

Can we train devout and gifted personnel for a television media world in which 92 percent of its professionals do not regularly attend church, 86 percent seldom or never attend, and 45 percent claim no religion at all? Should not the media frontier be a prime vocational target for the more than three out of ten Americans who do attend church weekly? A poll by *Public Opinion* magazine reveals that the media elite hold a strong liberal political bias and are one-sidedly on the left: 85 percent see nothing wrong with homosexual practice, 54 percent see nothing wrong with adultery. In matters of morality, the media elite are out of step with grassroots conviction; their program preferences and content reflect this more latitudinarian stance. What's more, sponsors do not prepare their own television programs; rather, programs guaranteeing a certain number of viewers bring in the sponsors (it takes thirty-five million viewers to keep a prime time TV show on the air). Is there not some way to exert a larger moral and spiritual influence? Could not character roles in television scripts become sufficiently human to include the spiritual concerns that impinge upon life? Why must the clergy appear mainly in a perfunctory way, to bless an unpromising marriage, for example, or to insert an inane bit of living room conversation, or to pronounce the benediction at a tragic funeral?

We need an evangelical task force fully aware that a cadre of influential intellectuals—one that constitutes only 15 percent of the population of the United States—largely shapes the thinking of government, business, education, and the media. However much the secular vanguard may caricature evangelical religion as balderdash, even the worst evangelical performance is just as cognitively illuminating and probably more so than modern culture generally. Even at their shoddiest, evangelicals retain at least some worldview sensibilities. Surely humanists more than evangelicals set the mood of prime time entertainment, whose philosophy is "give the public what it wants."

What vision do we have, what strategy, what program, what burden of prayer, what actual commitment to goals, that could change the larger outlook? The modern university world boasts scholars of magnificent academic credentials, yet to many of them the God of the Bible is as little known as was the confessedly "unknown god" of ancient Athens. To them as he did to the rabbi Nicodemus, Jesus would reiterate the absolute need of personal regeneration; he was no less interested, however, in the intellectual bearing of biblical theism on the whole span of learning, in love of the divine that enlists all of self in the service of God. Despite our costly disengagement from secular leadership, does not God in sovereign grace still turn towering agents to himself for spiritual witness in earlier ages, even as he did Saul of Tarsus and Augustine? Has he not gifted the church in every age—including our own—with kingdom spokesmen and pioneers?

From time to time Christian editors write incisive moral and spiritual commentary on national trends. I have long considered it tragic that we have been unable to mount a television panel that thrusts such convictions openly into the national debate. People properly look to editors rather than to evangelists for well-formulated criticism and guidance on public issues. I do not imply that evangelical legislators should be bypassed, but simply assume that Christian editors inform themselves about the merit of public proposals that specially concern the churches.

Besides the contribution made by editors of evangelical magazines and of book editors in religious publishing houses, we should also note that evangelicals holding key posts in the secular arena are familiar names throughout the media world. We mention only newscaster Steve Bell of ABC-TV, radio newscaster Paul Harvey, *Time* religion editor Richard Ostling, wire service religion editor George Cornell of AP, religion editor Russ Chandler of the *Los Angeles Times* and religion editor Bruce Buursma of the *Chicago Daily Tribune*, Forrest Boyd of International Media Service, and political correspondent Wes Pippert, now in Tel Aviv covering Israel for UPI.

In recent years thousands of graduate students have pursued doctorates in mass communications. Many of them aspire to hosting television panels or radio talk shows; perhaps fortunately only a small percentage will actually make the grade. But where are the evangelical aspirants to such public careers? Is it that evangelicals are not good conversationalists? Although we are on speaking terms with God, is our world too circumscribed, our overall knowledge too limited? We are weak if the intellectual band is so narrow that substance gives way to shallowness. A truly great talk show is not an exercise in fripperies. It is rather a soul-stretching experience in which spontaneous exchange between gifted interviewer and his or her guest carries the listeners to new vistas of information and insight.

We still wait for the evangelical colleges to formulate a television series that powerfully states and elaborates the biblical world-life view. What gain is it to hoard financial endowments in a decisive turning time when the whole intellectual heritage is under fire? Perhaps cable television and satellite-to-home television will emerge more and more as an alternative to present network restraints on evangelical visibility. As the third largest cable complex, the Christian Broadcasting Network, for example, already reaches a potential of over twenty-two million households, even if its programming is not exclusively religious.

It is ironical indeed that it took a grant from the National Endowment for the Humanities to spur a contingent of evangelical scholars to visit each other's campuses for shared presentation of worldview perspectives. The privately supported project of the Institute for Advanced Christian Studies to issue paperbacks that can reach beyond our own circles into the secular academic mainstream represents a broad evangelical effort. Even colleges once devoted to biblical distinctives that in time yielded to modernism and humanism are now concerned about the severe cultural shift to relativism and skepticism; some are open to an academic reprobing of the Judeo-Christian alternative. The secular campus on which I currently teach, for example, is inaugurating a Christian Studies program. Instead of viewing nonevangelical campuses only as alien, we should remember that liberal arts education was long regarded as preparatory to crowning courses in divinity, and that unless illumined by evangelical theism, all other disciplines of study remain incomplete and impoverished. It is all the more disconcerting when, as a member of a state legislature told me recently about his own experience, the teaching at some evangelical colleges differs hardly at all from that on secular campuses in areas where he had every right to expect an alternative.

I have not outlined a political agenda for evangelical editors to thrust upon the nation. Some who may want that would, I am confident, be among the first to reject it. This is an hour for us to share in the outworking of evangelical commonalities. A public relations specialist recently asked me whether the same foibles beset evangelical journalists as do secular journalists; they do not like to be left with questions, he said, but expect tidy, neatly-packaged answers that short-circuit thought. All the more, the world needs your carefully honed input. Surely by now we all take for granted the importance of evangelical involvement in public affairs. What we have not yet sorted out, amid fast-moving events in our pluralistic society, is the respective priority we should assign to clarification of principles and to concentration on action, and just what tolerances a consistent evangelical program ought or ought not to accommodate by way of political compromise.

Political action does not lend itself to a hurried implementation of the millennium; in truth, it is not a means to the millennium at all. But in the political order we must stand for social justice and clarify what social justice is (since the concept is not self-defining), and we must emphasize that the God of the Bible is the One who alone properly identifies it. After years of talk by national denominations about the needs of the poor, it is astonishing to learn that a study conducted by Senator Mark Hatfield's office shows that welfare programs could be eliminated in the United States if every church and synagogue assumed responsibility for just one family.

We have no mandate to theoretically legislate divine imperatives upon a pluralistic political realm. But we do have a duty to proclaim the revelatory truths and principles by which God will decisively judge every nation—and we must strive to advance them. If the ideas we affirm are spineless, if we bend biblical principles to accommodate one or another modern deviation, then what passes for evangelical behavior will soon obscure and even subvert revelatory perspectives and reinforce a sub-Christian society.

The present cultural upheaval is specially deleterious to the role of the family in society. In the context of the sexual revolution, liberation becomes a pseudonym for illicit sensuality that labels Judeo-Christian premises a primitive taboo. It will not be among the least of your virtues that you left a witness of personal fidelity in an age when monogamous marriage was under intense fire, and that you championed the right to life in a society that lauds hedonistic indulgence.

There are some gratifying signs of renaissance, far more good signs than we suspect. If each of us listed just two or three indicators of encouraging evangelical breakthrough known to us personally, we would be cheered that God is still on the move. Think only of the generosity with which people have responded to causes which not many years ago were but a prayer and a vision. I cannot vouch for its accuracy, but I have recently seen an estimate of $213 million as the combined budget of Jerry Falwell, Oral Roberts, Billy Graham, the 700 Club, and PTL. Add to this the budgets of Campus Crusade, World Vision, Prison Fellowship, *Christianity Today*, and certain other evangelical enterprises. Yet I sometimes wonder whether, for lack of larger coordination and comprehension, we have missed and continue to forego opportunities that will cost the younger generation dearly.

In a doctrinally drowsy moment not long ago, I daydreamed of a great evangelical publication—one that blended, among others, the best of *Christianity Today*, *Decision*, *World Vision*, *Christian Herald*, *Moody Monthly*, *Eternity*, and the *Reformed Journal*. One great evangelical magazine, like a spiritually reborn *Time* or *Newsweek*, I mused, would keep more than a million subscribers abreast of all the intellectual, spiritual, and ethical currents and would focus on theological priorities, moral matters, missionary and evangelistic gains and losses, humanitarian relief concerns, major book reviews, and current religious news events. Each participating effort would reinforce the others in their overlapping interests; each would make its own distinctive promotional appeals without duplicating what the rest were doing. Evangelicals would be challenged to a comprehensively global vision with appropriate priorities, and commonalities and differences would be stated with logical precision. The goal of this monolithic publication would be to strengthen evangelical vitality and perspective, and to steadily lift the reader to grasp world needs and opportunities.

Suddenly I realized that I am supposed to be a premillennialist and that everything is supposed to wax worse and worse rather than better. After all, I said, we already have *United Evangelical Action* (the quarterly, that is); we have *World Vision* and *Decision* once a month, we have Christianity fortnightly (nine or ten months a year anyway) or rather *Christianity Today* (although not really one day at a time), while the *Fundamentalist Journal* bids for tomorrow, and *Eternity* has preempted the day after tomorrow! Like third-world guerrillas, we often spray random machine gun bullets at the status quo and in so doing sometimes accidentally (and sometimes not so accidentally) hit each other. Perhaps we are not always sure who our friends are, and worse yet, not really sure who the enemy is. But if we, as God's press corps, find our true role in the cultural crossfire, we will turn our intimidating deadlines into innovative lifelines.

May God so will it.

"God's Press Corps in the Cultural Crossfire," Notes

1. Robert Bellah, "Religion in the University: Changing Consciousness, Changing Structures," in C. Welch, *Religion in the Undergraduate Curriculum: An Analysis and Interpretation* (Washington, D.C.: Association of American Colleges, 1972), 1318.

2. Carl Sagan, *Cosmos* (New York: Random House, 1980), 29, 257, 285.

What Commander Needs Tin Soldiers?

*I*n 2 Timothy, the apostle Paul exhorts young Timothy to be "a good soldier of Christ Jesus" (2:3). If you were telling a young soldier—your own brother, perhaps—to be on the alert, to keep his guard up, as we say, what advice would you give him?

Paul offers some pointed cautions about life in "the last days"—that is, life on earth in this whole interim period between the resurrection of Jesus and the Lord's return. He uses the phrase, "terrible times." In *A Tale of Two Cities*, Charles Dickens said: "It was the best of times, it was the worst of times, it was the age of wisdom, it was the age of foolishness, it was the epoch of belief, it was the epoch of incredulity, it was the season of Light, it was the season of Darkness, it was the spring of hope, it was the winter of despair." But Paul describes this present time as "terrible". The Greek term, in fact, means "furious" or "ferocious," and that is alarming enough to snap us to attention.

I want first to focus on the spiritual horizon that overhangs the conflict between vice and virtue, then to note the agenda of

Seventy-fifth annual commencement address to Point Loma Nazarene College graduates in San Diego, California, on 3 June 1985.

evils against which Paul warns us, and finally to offer a reminder that, in the spiritual struggle on which the direction of history now depends, our Commander in Chief needs more than tin soldiers. In the spirit of the great apostle, I urge each of us to live by the mighty truth and power of God, to live above the sludge of a sick society, and to live among dispirited humans as the vanguard of peace and good news.

1. *Live by the mighty truth and power of God.*

Paul clearly expects the young evangelical soldier to possess a *knowledge of the truth,* to be *a lover of God,* and to manifest *the power of godliness.* Take it from Paul's letter to young Timothy: if you are estranged from the truth, if you do not love God, and if you lack the power of godliness, your cause is a lost cause in these perilous times.

The world is full of religiosity. There are many varieties of it—Nazarene religiosity, Baptist religiosity, Episcopal religiosity, Methodist religiosity, Presbyterian religiosity, and ninety-nine other varieties. By "religiosity" I mean the outer appearance of religious vitality without the inner reality, a public piety "seen of men" to which even God shuts his eyes. Our Commander in Chief seeks recruits who love him and manifest "the power of godliness"; he wants informed and empowered recruits. No commander needs tin soldiers.

I do not for a moment question the great value of scientific studies or of liberal arts learning. What we know about the universe and what computer technology enables us today to do with such scientific data, lifts our generation head and shoulders above earlier generations. Yet the space-time relativities of modern science stand constantly in need of revision and updating. Empirical science is never able to reach absolute truth, because its observational data are incomplete. Worse yet, it cannot even deal with the supernatural or with moral absolutes, for these fall outside its area of competence.

Nor does philosophical reasoning decisively illumine the perennial problems of human thought and life. The great philosophers of the past and of the present blatantly contradict each other in their representations of truth and meaning. Like the Athenians of old, every generation pursues a vanguard of new intellectual frontiersmen which the next generation abandons in the name of intellectual progress.

Paul speaks of having knowledge of the truth. Jesus said, "You will know the truth, and the truth will set you free" (John 8:32). In the strictest sense, that truth is the redemption that is in Christ Jesus. Christ is himself "the way, the truth and the life" (John 14:6). Without him, sing the Jesus People, "there is no 'going' (to the Father); without him there is no 'knowing' (of the Father); and without him there is no 'living' (with the Father)." The theories for which our contemporaries hunger do not set men free; they leave mankind in moral chaos, in bondage to sin, and in the grip of death.

Among my acquaintances I count Dr. Calvin Linton, former president of Cosmos Club and dean of the college of liberal arts at George Washington University. In addressing an academic gathering recently, he made a pointed comment. "Christians do not know many absolutes, but they at least know some," he remarked, "and that places them far ahead of the skeptical relativists of our contemporary culture." Are you astride the scriptural revelation of the sovereign Creator, Redeemer, and Judge of this universe, of his holy commandments, of his grace in Christ? Are you aware that even if Western technology erupts into an unthinkably destructive nuclear war, God will still be there, and you will be there, and the Ten Commandments will be there, and all men and nations must appear at the judgment throne of Christ? It is in this context of overarching spiritual realities that Paul issues his warning against entrapments that a good soldier of Christ will avoid. *Live by the mighty truth and power of God.* Gain knowledge of the truth. Be a lover of God. Manifest the power of godliness. God has no use for tin soldiers.

2. *Live above the sludge of our sick society.*

Paul lists a whole agenda of evils—a catalog of colossal corruption illustrating the breakdown of moral law and the waning of cultural tradition that haunts those who tune their lives to this world. Twice he writes of misdirected love: "People will be lovers of themselves" (3:2) and shall be "lovers of pleasure" (v. 4). Paul is concerned about Timothy's love-life and yours, too. He knows that only if we put God first will we hold everything else in proper perspective. Human beings gripped only by religious formalism can be lured easily into the indecencies and immoralities and immodesties of the age. Without God first, natural affection goes (v. 3), parental obedience wanes (v. 2), covenant commitments are violated (v. 3). He speaks of lack of control over one's passions that results in unchastity. (v. 4)

What a shopping list of vices he charts: "lovers of money, boastful, proud, abusive, ungrateful, unholy, slanderous, without self-control, brutal, not lovers of the good, treacherous, rash, conceited." What is this but the unraveling warp and woof of a society that foregoes its right to survival? Paul knows how readily the faithless soldier forsakes his line of duty and goes AWOL. What starts out as mere "R and R"—rest and relaxation—moves from covetousness to include contempt for those who are good, and even turning traitor to one's cause. The unstable soldier not only will drift into the enemy camp; he soon leaves his heart there.

Live above the sludge of our sick society, Paul exhorts us. This world is unworthy of the Christian's heart. Perhaps you have read the recent book by Charles Colson, the post-Watergate convert, titled *Loving God.* Like a great many Watergate figures, Colson was a university graduate with an earned doctorate—in his case, law. You may not know that during the Watergate proceedings the American Association of University Professors considered a resolution to condemn the Watergate participants from Nixon on down for their moral insensitivity. But someone pointed out that all the main Watergate transgressors had graduated from mainline universities like those in which these very professors were teaching. The resolution was promptly withdrawn. You can graduate today from the most prestigious universities and not be a lover of God and the good. You can graduate even from Christian colleges and not love

God. But unless you love God, you will become mired in the sludge of our sick society.

Our century is the first in Western history that has sought to build human culture on the premise of the irrelevance of God. Moral imperatives, according to modern humanism, are mere culture prejudices; the Ten Commandments and the Sermon on the Mount are dismissed as fundamentalist fetishes. We are told that, since Freud has explained our psychoses, the sense of sin and guilt need no longer trouble us moderns; since Marx has sketched the world's future in terms of final communist takeover, we need not take seriously the ancient prophets! Yet the generation that now walks in the shadow of these secular myths has lost the meaning and worth of human survival. Our educated young intellectuals have a higher suicide rate than their less learned contemporaries. The century that was heralded as the dawning of world brotherhood and of universal peace is dusking under a mushroom cloud of international apprehension. We have lost our way, and darkness is falling over our heady civilization.

You have no reason, Paul says, to be swept away by the wild winds of worldly rebellion. Help our generation find a new constellation of critical concern. The torch of morality and conscience, of love and compassion, of freedom and hope, needs to be refueled. *Live by the mighty truth and power of God. Live above the sludge of our sick society.*

3. *Live in a dispirited age as the vanguard of peace and good news.*

You can be part of a strategic alliance who take God and moral absolutes and divine truth seriously; you can lead in the renewing of our crumbling society. The cause of justice and peace in society is a noble one, and evangelicals should be in the forefront of it. There will be no real peace without man's reconciliation to God and without reconciliation to one's fellowman; all else is simply a delay of hostilities or a tenuous cold war. That is worthwhile, to be sure, in an age of missile-launching powers.

But it is one of the perversities of our age that most educational institutions no longer recognize the importance of the Bible and of the Judeo-Christian revelation. Some of our greatest centers of learning emphasized at their beginnings what they now obscure at the peak of their influence. Not unlike many other major educational institutions, Harvard University in its original charter contained this statement: "Let every student well consider . . . that the main end of his life and studies is to know God and Jesus Christ." Human theorizing and experience once bowed—and needs once again to bow—in the presence of a reality infinitely greater than this universe, the reality of the living God, a transcendent reality whose mystery is dispelled by God's intelligible self-revelation and his incarnation in Jesus Christ.

Live among dispirited humans as the vanguard of peace and good news. You can do that if clothed in the armor that God provides. Remember Paul's exhortation: "Our fight is not against human foes, but against cosmic powers, against the authorities and potentates of this dark world, against the superhuman forces of evil in the heavens. Therefore, take up God's armor; then you will be able to stand your ground when things are at their worst, to complete every task and still to stand" (Ephesians 6:12-14, NEB). "Be a good soldier of Christ Jesus," Paul exhorts Timothy (2:3); "continue in what you have learned and have become convinced of" (3:14).

You know a constellation of imperishable values. *Live by the mighty truth and power of God. Live above the sludge of a sick society. Live among dispirited humans as the vanguard of peace and good news.*

Remember, our Commander in Chief has no use for tin soldiers.

Scripture Index

Subject Index

147